Praise for *If God Is Love,*

"John asserts that he is a 'longtime Christian by aspiration (if not always in practice),' and his book demonstrates how his choices—his practice—have matched that aspiration repeatedly, even when he's sad, angry, or disillusioned. John's compassion, humanity, humility, and humor are present throughout. His candor is authentic, and his inspiration accessible and also challenging, in the very best sense. This is a book for anyone on a journey of faith or a journey of service, whether or not those two, as they do for John, intertwine—or for anyone who loves a terrific read."
— Chelsea Clinton, author and advocate

"With clarity and candor, John reminds us of the compassion at the heart of what it means to be a spiritual human being and offers a loving expression of faith that is so necessary right now. *If God Is Love, Don't Be a Jerk* calls us to create a more just and equitable world—one that affirms the beauty in all humanity—and leaves us feeling that it is all within our hands."
— Yvette Nicole Brown, actress, writer, and activist

"John Pavlovitz is the real thing. His compassion, empathy, wisdom, and guts will remind you of what Jesus actually preached. This self-described 'theological mutt' is a pastor, a prophet, a poet, and a prince. John has given us a book of great insight and wit. It will remind you of what Christianity is supposed to be about. I can't wait to give it as a gift."
—John Fugelsang, comedian, writer, and political commentator

"John gives us a road map to take the best parts of our religious beliefs and find a space for reconciliation, compassion, and kindness—not just for others but for ourselves. John's bold, unwavering voice encourages us to find our common ground and, together, to rise up against bigotry and hatred."

—Amy Siskind, activist and author

"John Pavlovitz is an artisan of words. He's a poet and a provocateur. Like the prophet Jeremiah, he's got a fire 'shut up in his bones' that has to come out. That fire is love. But the love he writes about is not the sentimental love of storybooks and fairy tales and greeting cards. It is the harsh and dreadful love that Dostoyevsky spoke of—the love that caused Jesus to flip tables in the temple, the love that got the prophets killed, the love that led the freedom fighters to jail and the martyrs to be burned at the stake. The love John writes about is the love that keeps us up at night because there are folks still out on the streets while we have an extra room in our homes. It is the love that cuts with the precision of a surgeon's scalpel, because before we can get better, we have to cut out the cancer that made us sick. Enjoy this book, and let it mess with you."

—Shane Claiborne, author, activist,
and cofounder of Red Letter Christians

IF GOD IS LOVE, DON'T BE A JERK

IF GOD IS LOVE, DON'T BE A JERK

Finding a Faith That Makes Us Better Humans

JOHN PAVLOVITZ

WJK WESTMINSTER
JOHN KNOX PRESS
LOUISVILLE • KENTUCKY

First Edition
Published by Westminster John Knox Press
Louisville, Kentucky

21 22 23 24 25 26 27 28 29 30—10 9 8 7 6 5 4 3 2 1

Book design by Drew Stevens and Allison Taylor
Cover design by Allison Taylor

Library of Congress Cataloging-in-Publication Data is on file
at the Library of Congress, Washington, DC.

ISBN-13: 978-0-664-26684-4

PRINTED IN THE UNITED STATES OF AMERICA

♾ The paper used in this publication meets the minimum requirements
of the American National Standard for Information Sciences—Permanence
of Paper for Printed Library Materials, ANSI Z39.48-1992.

Most Westminster John Knox Press books are available at special
quantity discounts when purchased in bulk by corporations,
organizations, and special-interest groups. For more information,
please e-mail SpecialSales@wjkbooks.com.

This book is dedicated with gratitude
and affection to Jen, Noah, and Selah.

Thank you for loving me so well,
even when I'm a jerk.

CONTENTS

Introduction

YOU HAD ONE JOB

Love is the greatest force in the universe. It is the
heartbeat of the moral cosmos. He who loves is a
participant in the being of God.

—Rev. Dr. Martin Luther King Jr.

If you want a good laugh, Google the phrase "You had one
job." The results are a hilariously tragic parade of seemingly
impossible fails, unfathomably poor planning, and facepalm-
inducing human error: a piece of melted cheese on *top* of
a fast-food burger bun, the word "STOP" misspelled on a
street crossing, a "Keep to the Right" sign with its arrow facing left, a toilet lid inexplicably installed *below* the seat itself.
Seeing these stupefying train wrecks in task execution tends
to elicit two responses: usually making you feel a little bit
better about yourself while simultaneously wanting to track
down the culprits in an effort to understand how they managed to neglect the primary duty assigned to them. We begin
to speculate: Were they temporarily distracted? Did they
not properly comprehend the instructions? Did they feel
as though someone above them in the chain of command
dropped the ball? Were they just plain lazy? When people
miss the point so spectacularly, we want to know how and
why—because that kind of failure feels impossible from the

outside. It seems unfathomable to get the main thing wrong, and seeing it happen sparks our curiosity. I imagine Jesus knows well the curiosity that comes with watching people given clear direction lose their way.

As a longtime Christian by aspiration (if not always in practice), I often envision an exasperated Jesus coming back, and the first words out of his mouth to his followers as his feet hit the pavement being "You had one job: *Love*.[1] So, what happened?" I wonder what massive wave of excuses and rationalizations would come flooding from the mouths of the faithful multitude in front of him, how they might justify their mistreatment of the assailed humanity in their care, the verbal and theological gymnastics they'd attempt to avoid culpability for their own cruelty. Would they stridently recite him a verse from Leviticus? Would they blame the Liberal Media for morally corrupting America? Would they talk about people's wicked lifestyle choices? Would they argue that they *were* loving the sinners in their midst but simply hating their sin? Would they frantically offer up the same platitudes and parrot back the same partisan talking points they'd gotten used to brandishing on social media and proffering in Sunday school classes? And, if all else failed to convince him—would they quote Jesus to himself in a desperate Hail Mary effort to pass the buck to him for what they did or failed to do while supposedly standing in for him? And there, fully seen in the piercing gaze of the namesake of their very faith tradition, with all their justifications and excuses exhausted and only their fully exposed hearts left—would any of their responses be sufficient reasons for refusing to *love*, when that was the singular task and primary commandment that he left them responsible for tending to?

In my less compassionate moments, I admit that I like to picture it not going well for them. I know it's far less than admirable (let alone Christlike), but some days my heart strangely warms at the possibility of a few billion brimstone-breathing evangelists, sanctimonious conservative politicians, and plank-eyed[2] judgmental Christian neighbors all having to explain themselves in a sanctified flop-sweat moment they can't exegete or gaslight themselves out of, and they all get what they have coming to them—but my self-righteous revelry doesn't last long. The mirror calls me out as I remember what I think I know about Jesus, and that rescues me from full-blown, unabated hubris. I begin to wonder what *my* excuses might be, how I'd spin the enmity I manufacture here, what story I'd come up with for not doing the one task we both know comprises a disciple's job description. And if I really believe what I'm supposed to believe, are any of my justifications sufficient? If God *is* love and if Jesus is the perfect expression *of* that love and if I am supposedly trying to follow that Jesus—how can I be so love-impaired so frequently? How do I miss the singular point so consistently?

It's not as if I didn't know what I was signing up for, like some lengthy online user agreement I blindly accepted in haste, missing the bombshell fine print beneath. Having read the Gospels a few million times (give or take a few hundred thousand), I know the primary commandment is not something I need to excavate from cumbersome layers of foreign language translations and cultural mores of the time. Jesus himself clearly laid out the most important commandment for me and for everyone who's ever cracked open a Bible (and even most people who haven't but know the story anyway), so we'd all understand what's being asked of us going in; so there would be no post-altar-call buyer's remorse or deathbed claims of a sucker-punch bait and switch. Loving *God* and *neighbor* and *self* is the elemental stuff of Christian prayers, songs, T-shirts, and bumper stickers—and we know that. But as the master Morpheus said to protégé Neo in the first (and only truly great) *Matrix* film, "There is a difference between knowing the path and walking the path."[3] Love is the path that Jesus laid out for us. I'm going to assume we agree on that, and we won't waste a lot of time arguing it here. This book is about the *walking:* about imagining what love should or could look like if we take that mandate seriously, about whatever it is that interrupts and derails us along the way. It's about the ways a bigger God is going to yield a greater capacity to love more people, and about what that stretching will cause us to confront and confess and jettison. It's going to be eventually beautiful but not always pleasant along the way. It's no fun to face your failures, and I speak from a wealth of experience.

Throughout my life, I've often imagined I was a Christian. I was raised in a Christian home and went to a Christian school. After a few meandering spiritual wilderness years as a skeptical but hopeful agnostic, I attended a Christian seminary, became a Christian pastor, and have served in Christian churches for most of the past twenty-five years of my life. (Not enough *Christian* for you? No problem, I've got more.) Along the way, I've read and studied and preached the Scriptures extensively; led community Bible studies and student retreats and overseas mission trips; ministered in tiny, rural chapels and massive, gleaming megachurches. I've crisscrossed the country for the better part of five years, sharing the Good News as I understand it. I've done all the religious *stuff* that proper Christians are supposed to do. As a result of these decades immersed in this tradition both personally and vocationally, I thought that I at least had the gist of Jesus, that I was in the blessed ballpark. Now, I think

I might have been doing this wrong all these years. Maybe I assumed something that I shouldn't have, because much of the time I don't quite feel like I fit in the places professed Jesus-folk gather.

I always thought Christians were supposed to care about people—not necessarily agree with them or believe what they believe or even like them, but to see them each as specific and unique image-bearers of the Divine, and to want to work for *shalom* for them: wholeness, happiness, peace, safety, rest—regardless of where they came from or what they believed or who they loved. I grew up believing that one of the markers of a life that emulated Jesus was a pliable heart capable of being broken at the distress of other human beings: when they are hungry and hurting, when they are homeless and afraid, when they grieve and feel alone, when they believe they are unloved and forgotten, when tragedy befalls them, and when injustice assails them. These things are supposed to move the needle within us if Jesus is softening our hearts, or at least I imagined so.

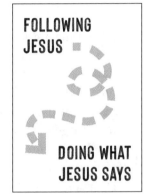

FOLLOWING JESUS

DOING WHAT JESUS SAYS

Even in seasons of defiance and doubt, when I wasn't sure that Jesus was who they said he was or that I believed anything about salvation and damnation, I took that *love your neighbor* business seriously. In those obstinate, back-sliding seasons of rebellion when I was what true disciples call a hopelessly lost sheep, I was sure that compassion was nonnegotiable for Jesus followers. I always knew sacrificial love was the narrow road and the better path, that loveless Christianity was an oxymoron—and that if I ever claimed faith, I'd better be more loving than if I didn't. I bet you know all that too, which is why you're in disbelief that so many professed Christians neglect the one job of loving people, and why you're compelled to get it right. We need such human beings walking around now more than ever, given where we're headed, at least in America.

I'm writing these words in the last days of a COVID-ravaged, racism-scarred, election-battered 2020 that seems determined to squeeze in every bit of disaster it can before angrily departing into the annals of history, future therapy bills, and the recurring nightmares of everyone who managed to live through it. Here, in this current disorienting maelstrom of prolonged isolation, wild conspiracy theories, election fraud claims (and other assorted personal and national disasters too lengthy to list here), there are a whole lot of things I *don't* know. I don't know if I'll spend a second birthday in quarantine. I don't know if my kids will homeschool through college. I don't know if I'll ever get to use my frequent flyer miles. I don't know if before the end of the year, Donald Trump is going to declare Mar-a-Lago a sovereign nation and himself its rightful king.

But there *is* one thing about the future I do know right now, one coming reality that I can safely predict with 100 percent certainty regardless of who assumes or retains the presidency, what the composition of Congress turns out to be, or whether there is a blue or a red majority in America: loveless, Jesus-less Christianity is going to leave us fractured in ways we've never been before. There is going to be relational collateral damage in families, faith communities will be broken apart, lifelong friendships will be irreparably harmed, injustice will be prevalent—and hateful religion will have compounded it all. No political result of November 3, 2020, was going to change what was true on the day before, or on the day I'm writing these words, or on the day you're reading them. The calendar and the politicians are immaterial. These injuries we're tending to are all far bigger than partisan politics or national election results, and they won't be relegated to a single calendar year either. These are evergreen afflictions.

For as long as human beings have been declaring devotion to a God of love, they have been gloriously screwing it up by being hateful in the process. The Bible doesn't shy away from that, and neither should we. If we've been paying attention, we know that for as much as religion has bent the arc of the moral universe toward justice,[4] it has just as often pulled it into inequity. For whatever liberation has come via the people of Jesus, we have collectively engineered bondage and fortified supremacy as well. It's good to admit this as we try to fashion something better from what has been. It's necessary to see the ugly things in the shadowed places of our nation and in our faith tradition as we work to let a little bit of light in. That isn't going to be as easy or as neat or as comfortable as we'd like.

I can understand why you might not want to accept the invitation I'm offering here. (Lord literally knows, I've avoided it for most of my life.) It's a fairly simple and painless task to identify the people out there who we believe are doing religion wrong and condemn them. We can usually accomplish that with very little effort. And though it's a bit less pleasant, we might even be willing to document the ways and times in which we respond poorly to people and to circumstances. It is a far more invasive and disruptive endeavor to pause long enough and dig deep enough to consider what we actually believe and how that belief shapes our dispositions and directs our paths. That process leaves a mark. Most of us aren't looking for an existential crisis—but let's be willing to have one: to admit our questions, inventory our struggles, and attend to our burdens. (You're likely having such a crisis whether you acknowledge it or not, otherwise you wouldn't be here.) And since you are, you're probably in some form of deconstruction, reconstruction, or straight-up demolition of your former faith. You are in the emotional growing pains of adult spirituality. Reexamining your entire image of God is going to be a bit of an interruption, something you can't numb with a streaming binge or a couple hours of mindless slot-machine scrolling through your newsfeed. When your previous understanding of whatever you imagine set life into motion and holds it all together and directs your movements faces disturbance, there are going to be consequences and costs and collateral damage. Many people don't want to do that invasive, uncomfortable work, which is why they're satisfied allowing someone else to tell them what to believe.

I'm glad that, for whatever reason, you're not satisfied with that. Our world, starved for love, is glad too.

Chapter 1
UNBOXING GOD

"Oh, no—I'm trapped in these pants."

That was the first thought I had as I careened wildly around my walk-in closet. It probably sounds as ridiculous to you now as it did in my head in that moment. The situation had deteriorated rapidly. Just five minutes earlier I'd been quietly thumbing through the outer reaches of my clothes rack, far from the well-traveled middle section, where outfits no longer suitable for respectable humans languish for years in dust and darkness before finally being evicted into cardboard boxes or garbage bags and sentenced to spend their remaining days in the attic or garage. As a series of once-sensible (and now tragically laughable) fashion decisions slid past me, I stopped abruptly as I suddenly found myself face-to-face with a thirty-year-old friend: a pair of ladies' stretch denim pants I'd purchased in 1988 at the Cherry Hill Mall in southern New Jersey. (Author's note: I was twenty years old, had a long and luxurious mane of thick, naturally curly chestnut hair—and as the male singer in a local "hair band," as they were affectionately known, there was absolutely nothing unusual about buying my clothes in a women's clothing store.) As I stared reverently at the glorious acid-washed relic of my youth gone wild, suddenly a voice in my head that strongly resembled my own said, "You know, I bet they still fit." Like the crafty serpent tempting Adam and Eve in the garden, the voice dared me forward. "Go ahead . . . try them on." At fifty-one years old, I still consider myself in pretty good shape, so I answered back with naive optimism, "Why not?"

I was about to get a definitive answer.

Things started off promisingly enough. I bent down and grabbed the waistband, stepped into the small leg holes that easily traversed my ankles, but by the time I reached my calves I realized I was in trouble as progress slowed substantially. Undaunted, I doubled my resolve and pressed on (which turned out to be a really terrible idea). I was soon wriggling wildly and my breathing became noticeably labored as I tried to muscle myself all the way into what had quickly become a pair of pale blue human sausage casings. When those efforts proved futile, I began to hop violently like a stationary sack-race participant, hoping the blunt force of gravity would thrust my thighs the rest of the way through the now obviously woefully undersized space provided. After four or five desperate heaves, I felt a rush of air suddenly vacuum-sealing me in, and mercifully came to rest on the ground. I stood there with my chest heaving and forehead perspiring, as if having just completed high-intensity cardio training, and initially feeling pleased with myself—however, any satisfaction was only a momentary victory, as I felt the elastic waistband sharply digging into my skin and my legs started to quickly lose feeling due to lack of blood flow. It was then that I came to three sobering realizations: (1) I was no longer twenty years old, (2) I still hadn't fully exhaled, and (3) I wasn't getting out of these pants by myself.

They say that the first step in getting help of any kind is admitting that you have a problem. I could tell from the substantial tension my lower extremities were under that if

I'd tried to sit down in that moment, I'd surely have set off a powerful explosion, sending spandex shrapnel into every corner of our walk-in closet. In a welcome moment of sober humility, I reluctantly called for help. Hearing my distant, muffled cries for assistance, my wife and kids came running in from other rooms of the house, expecting from the desperation in my voice that I'd had a bad fall or heart episode—and instead were greeted by a grown man imprisoned by his own pair of ladies' slacks. After they helped to extricate me, we all had a good laugh at my expense, and when sensation returned to my legs, I placed the pants (which had now shrunken back to their original size) back on the hanger. I wasn't ready to say good-bye to them just yet.

If I had expired there in that closet, my cause of death would have been listed as *Unintentional Spandecide caused by reckless arrogance.* It would have been a classic case of user error. No one would have blamed the pants. They may have functioned back when I bought them, but they certainly weren't designed to contain me thirty years and four inches of girth later. I wasn't supposed to fit into them any longer and shouldn't have tried. That's how you find yourself in peril in your bedroom closet.

This has been my spiritual journey over the past decade and a half: trying desperately to cram my belief into a space it was no longer capable of fitting into, hoping that sheer will, a little denial, and lots of wishful thinking would allow me to stay in something I'd long outgrown but couldn't quite bring myself to admit did not fit anymore. There's a song church people have sung together for decades: *Gimme that ol' time religion, it's good enough for me.* (Far from a ringing endorsement, by the way.) But what do you do when that ol' time religion *isn't* good enough for you anymore, when *good enough* is far less than what you are seeking in the deepest recesses of your heart? If I'm honest, the further I've walked into my adult life and the more open I've been to being surprised and to changing my mind and to considering better stories about spiritual things, the more organized religion has been an exercise in diminishing returns: God getting progressively bigger, while the space I'd once created to contain that God grows more and more restrictive, more and more suffocating. When you find yourself in that newly confining space, the fear and the guilt can be overwhelming, and it can make you freeze. For years as a local church pastor I stayed where I was (literally and figuratively), either because I thought

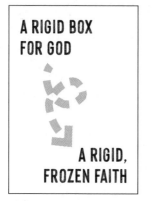

A RIGID BOX FOR GOD

A RIGID, FROZEN FAITH

something might give if I prayed hard enough, or maybe because I was too terrified to confront the reality that my faith was shifting—but the pressure was profound and constant. Something that was supposed to be life-giving suddenly became difficult to breathe inside of.

You don't need to be a pastor or a Christian to understand spiritual claustrophobia, because it is consistent in all existential crises, and it's more common than most of us admit or realize. In my travels both online and around the country, I meet thousands of similarly *squeezed* people: human beings who still passionately crave the wide-open wonder of genuine spiritual pursuits and the transformative spaces of loving community, but who aren't finding those things in the religious stories and systems and buildings of their childhoods. Now that they're getting older, they're taking off the no longer useful hand-me-down theologies they inherited and looking something that fits them today. These days, Sundays are different for them, church is different, and God is different, but the yearning is still there and the burdens still twist their insides. They may be losing their ol' time religion, but they haven't lost their hunger to find sacred spaces, to confront the persistent questions, to live in justice communities, to see realities deeper than the surface, or to participate in something greater than themselves—and this is where the journey to a more loving religion begins: embracing the questions, discarding old stories, being humble enough to start again.

Whenever people say, "I'm spiritual but not religious," this is usually another way of saying, "I've outgrown my God box and am currently looking for a bigger one." They're telling you that they've either willingly left or been evicted from the place they once called home, the geography of their former faith. They are wandering prodigals either by choice or by necessity. They may have discovered an irreconcilable difference with a theological position in their faith tradition or grown exhausted from a silent response to injustice from the pews, or they simply woke up one day and realized they can't pray the prayers they used to—and something has to give. I think most honest people of faith, every sincere sojourner, and lots of introspective human beings who are pressed up against the profound mysteries of this life (and whatever might happen beyond its conclusion) are looking for a bigger God and for a tangible expression of goodness that feels proportional to that God. We all want something *unbelievable* to believe in—something that is so massive and so capable of surprising us that it is always just slightly out of reach and just a little beyond our capacity to comprehend—and we want something that makes us and the people around us better humans. If not, it's probably not worth our time.

The moment someone tells you they have this spiritual life figured out, that's a red flag that they're lying to you or to themselves. This book is for the rest of us: the restless, the unsettled, the unconvinced, and even the downright defiantly opposed; for people who want more love than they've encountered in organized religion. I think if we're doing faith right, we're supposed to be there. Evolving spirituality will always give people the desire to shed the skins of their current belief system, always push them to outgrow their present assumptions about the world, and it will forever be increasing their capacity for change. That expansion is necessary. But narrow religion will usually shrink everything over time—until one day it all blows up.

A few months ago I got a frantic email from my friend Tiffany, who said she needed to talk as soon as possible. This was out of character for her, and the unusual urgency of her message moved me to reach for the phone. "I'm in free fall," she said almost immediately, and continued quickly, her voice breaking, "I feel like I have no ground to stand on right now." Then there was silence, broken only by quiet sniffs. I knew a good deal of Tiffany's backstory: a lifelong evangelical, raised Southern Baptist in Texas, she always had a tidy, clearly defined God box and a go-to set of Scriptures she wielded like a rudimentary first-aid kit for herself and others. In college she'd met Scott, a local student pastor, and—like a good, respectable Southern Baptist girl—soon became a Southern Baptist pastor's wife. For years everything was perfect (or at least, it worked for her given the story they'd told themselves), until she began to see hairline cracks forming in the bedrock of what she once believed. Their senior pastor's increasingly incendiary messages about the evils of the "gay agenda" and her church's silence in response to a new wave of bathroom-bill legislation started to conflict with the LGBTQ people she'd met and come to love. As so often happens as we grow and get better stories, life begins to argue with our theology—and Tiffany was in the middle of that increasingly heated disagreement with her former self. Over the past few years, she'd gradually cut many of the tethers of her previous religious narrative, which at first felt freeing; that is, until her marriage began to go south and her youngest daughter became very sick. In the past, during times of emotional, financial, and relational crisis, she'd gone to the familiar religious places of refuge—and they weren't cutting it any longer.

Tiffany said, "Before, when things fell apart, my (very specific) faith story was the thing I could hold on to. My image of God, my go-to Bible verses, those default prayers, the fallback platitudes, and my church family were all comforting." Her voice grew more desperate as sobs interrupted her. "Now that I don't have those things—what do I turn to? To people? To myself? To medication? I don't know what to anchor myself to anymore! I just feel like I'm drifting here."

Tiffany was feeling the growing pains of an expanding spirituality, of outgrowing the box. She'd let go of the restrictive religious doctrine of her childhood and early adulthood and found that the tiny theological container was no longer big enough for her beliefs, but in a time of trauma she'd struggled to find a suitable replacement. She was and is living with a new disorientation—one we should probably get used to.

If we're going to find a bigger God, one that makes us more loving, we have to admit and address two fundamental realities. The first is that *small religion is a problem*. It is the culprit of the suffocation and the source of our frustration because it tends to thrive on separation and breed exclusion. We've all seen and experienced small religion, so that may be the easier of the two truths to reckon with. The second and much more challenging reality is that *all religion is small religion*: yours, mine, that of the people you admire and those you can't stand, the traditions you hold tightly to and the ones you've long ago rejected. A God our brains and buildings can fully hold just isn't big enough to be truly God. The moment we imagine a rigid box adequately capable of containing the *who, what, how,* and *why* of everything that is or ever was or ever might be is the moment we've shrunken all the answers to the elemental questions down into something that is no longer God-sized. If we can fully fathom it, it ceases to be worthy of our reverence.

In writing to his church two thousand years ago and to those who would follow them in this journey, the apostle Paul writes a prayer that we as people of faith might "grasp how wide and long and high and deep is the love of Christ, and to know this love that surpasses knowledge—that you may be filled to the measure of all the fullness

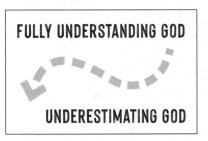

FULLY UNDERSTANDING GOD

UNDERESTIMATING GOD

of God."[1] That seems like both a beautiful aspiration and an impossible task. If there is no mystery left in our belief system, we need to move into a space that will accommodate it. No matter how fervently we've prayed, how earnestly we've searched, how diligently we've studied, or how sure of ourselves we currently are—we're either partially or substantially wrong. Whatever God is made of, we don't have the capacity to capture it completely in the minds we're equipped with. No religious tradition, no specific denomination, and certainly no single human being can fit it. It's all outdated, tight pants that can't hold the intended occupant. It isn't easy for good religious people to admit this, especially when most of us have been raised with *certainty* as a virtue and *doubt* as a mortal sin. We've been conditioned not only to believe, but to do so without hesitation or reservation or alteration—but that was never really the plan or the expectation. Jesus was surrounded by people who couldn't banish disbelief even with him close enough to touch, human beings who struggled to love people well even with a tangible example in front of them. We should probably give ourselves a break for struggling with two thousand years between us.

My formative religious tradition has been Christianity, and you'll hear many references to Jesus and to the stories of the Bible here, but this isn't about us matching theologically; it's about each of us stretching to reach a more expansive, more compassionate place than we started— which it turns out was always the point. The New Testament records Jesus teaching people about needing to put his "new wine" teaching into "new wineskins," not the brittle, rigid old ones they'd been used to.[2] He was asking people to have minds pliable enough and imaginations limber enough to consider a God beyond the one they currently believed in or the systems they inherited—and to extend themselves to people they'd never have lovingly engaged before. Much of his initial audience was a group of devout and oppressed Jewish believers who'd been patiently waiting hundreds of years for what they expected to be a conquering warrior to forcibly deliver them from generations of captivity and oppression. By asking them to embrace a poor, itinerant street preacher who asked them to be "servants of all," Jesus was inviting them into a disappointing, shocking—but necessary—heresy. His revolutionary movement of sacrificial love often involved him laying out a contrast between religious people's old story and the better one he was writing for them: "You have heard it said . . . But I tell you . . ."[3] Jesus' gentle challenge has always pulled those of us willing to listen into the discomfort that comes with expanding our understanding of just how big a love we're talking about here and what the implications are for us: the way we live and move through the world, the kind of audacious kindness we're being asked to practice.

At first, all this religious rethinking feels like a betrayal, like spiritual rebellion, and many times we resist it in order to stay in the comfort of surety and free from guilt, but there is something life-giving outside of where we started. Our initial faith traditions are all valid and meaningful. They can give us a working language with which to speak about the mysteries of this life, but whoever and whatever God is doesn't *require* them. Religion isn't necessarily bad or corrupt or unhelpful (often quite the contrary), but it is always undersized for the task at hand. Religion does its best to give us words for describing something that words aren't ultimately equipped for. Jesus wasn't asking people to register for a religion but inviting them into a way of being in the world individually and collectively, a way of being that is rooted in a propulsive love for humanity. I've grown to feel really sorry for people whose religion seems settled and finished, those who've so systematized and shrunken their spirituality that they no longer question or dream or imagine more.

You were born without a box for God. You probably know this even if you've forgotten it: that you met God before you ever had a religious container. You experienced beauty and wonder without needing church or a Bible verse or a pastor to explain it to you, and you don't need that now. I'm not necessarily telling you to abandon your faith tradition or that it's unhealthy for you—but I *am* telling you that your faith tradition is ultimately incomplete, and that it alone cannot house whatever it is that holds us all together. To admit this isn't a theological mutiny, it's finding the necessary humility to embrace something bigger than even your preferred box. Your own evolution testifies to the inevitability of outgrowing your former self. You probably don't believe what you believed twenty, ten, or even five years ago. (I sure hope you don't.) You've likely come to a fundamentally different understanding of things like climate change or immigration or same-sex marriage or the death penalty, as you've developed new relationships, accrued more life experiences, and been informed by exposure to new ideas. Hopefully you've undergone some kind of perspective transformation, because if not, that likely means you haven't learned anything new in that time. Spirituality should be a continual unfolding. New information will always alter our worldview, always challenge our assumptions, always move us from a former deeply entrenched position—and it will surprise us by coming without the old packaging.

Recently, I took a three-day writing retreat at a beach here in North Carolina. The ocean is medicinal for me. It helps quiet the noises that normally reside in my head, all the swirling worries and fears and obligations and bad news. As always, I waited to head down to the shoreline until late in the day when the sun began to descend and most people had headed to their houses and hotel rooms after a long and draining day of UV ray absorption. This timing usually allows me to have much of the beach to myself, and for an Olympic-level introvert who spends a good deal of time in front of crowds, the distance is often welcomed. I stepped through the dunes with a backpack and canvas chair over my shoulder, fully expecting to see a vast expanse of open sand and water—and instead was greeted by a group of forty or fifty people stretched in a line from the dunes to the shoreline. Curiosity immediately pulled me toward them, and soon I could see that they were all looking down at a single spot at their feet and realized what it was. I had almost literally stumbled upon an imminent sea turtle hatching. A few seconds later I found my place in the impromptu receiving line and knelt in the sand, shoulder to shoulder with strangers, my head a few inches from the narrow trench volunteers had recently carved out—and waited.

For two hours there was no discernible movement, until suddenly an infinitesimal shift in the grains on the surface, then another, and another. And almost immediately, dozens of tiny black shapes lit only by the moon broke through the ground and made their first, awkward journey into the relentless, churning ocean while fifty strangers quietly cheered them on. There were tears and hugs and high fives and applause all around. I didn't get much writing done. I didn't get alone time. I didn't make any progress on this book. I didn't get the solitary night I planned. I got something better.

Religious people often talk about the *thin places,* those rare moments when the wall between humanity and divinity becomes like onion skin and we can see through to something beyond. At this moment, this small patch of sand, water, and moonlight was that transparently sacred. This was a holy moment, a sudden clearing in the clouds.

Without a hymn or a prayer or a pew or a minister, God felt present and close. It was a *religious experience* in the greatest sense of the words. It couldn't be quantified or contained, and the overwhelming peace of the moment can't be accurately described as much as I'd like to. This was God unboxed. It was divinity digging itself from the sand. It was a beautiful upsizing, breaking out of the shell. You know what that feels like, don't you—an awe that escapes description and explanation?

LESS RELIANCE ON A BUILDING

AN EXPANDED SANCTUARY

When we experience moments that we identify as spiritual or miraculous or transcendent, they're seldom attached to organized religion or a single building, and rarely confined to a church service or Bible study. There is no doorway we need to walk through or threshold we need to cross to encounter the breathtaking stuff of butterflies and goose bumps. Despite our religious worldview or our practiced theology, we can all recognize a kind of sacredness in the disparate experiences of this life: standing in a crowd singing along to a band we love or hiking alone through a sunlit mountain pass or tasting food so delicious that it generates an involuntary sound of gastronomic adoration from somewhere deep within us. We know firsthand through art and music and love and sex and nature and relationship that there is a "thing" beyond the thing, that this life isn't only what we can see and feel and taste. The less dependent we are on a building for an hour on Sunday to replicate the transcendent encounter we have as we live through this life, the more we are able to understand the world as sacred, to embrace the truth that the place where we stand is always holy ground—that we are forever in the thin places if we pay attention. When you begin to unbox God, you may find yourself uncomfortable in church or religion because these places begin to feel restrictive to your soul. The prayers might no longer ring as true, the creeds may seem unwieldy, and the sermons start to sound alarms of hypocrisy. These are the growing pains of realizing that whatever holds this life together is a bit bigger than the old story you were taught and memorized; it goes beyond the borders that you'd mapped out. That's when you discover that God has left the building and that maybe you need to as well.

Chapter 2
SCARY BEDTIME STORIES

One of the initial and primary dilemmas we face when signing on to belief in a divine presence on any level is deciding the character and agenda of that presence: Is it fundamentally for me or against me? Am I safe in its company, or is my punishment imminent? Am I beloved by it as I am, or is its affection for me contingent upon my behavior or my belief? The answers to those questions are usually passed down to us before we can ever remember receiving them, which is why they're so hard to see objectively.

Growing up as a good little Catholic boy, I can remember inhaling the pungent incense hanging in the air of our massive Gothic sanctuary, kneeling into a soft red velvet pew pad, resting my elbows on the hard, polished wooden seat in front of me, and staring up into a cavernous stone and stained-glass canopy—praying to a God who spoke light and shape into being and numbered the very hairs on my head, a God who fully adored me but whose anger was never far away. I knew that I was loved completely, as long as I didn't screw it up in the infinite number of ways it seemed possible to do so: stealing, lying, masturbating, listening to Ozzy Osbourne, or one day voting Democrat. As a result, I often prayed, "Whom shall I fear?" while being rightly terrified. I was taught that God was both steadfast in love and easily angered, and no adults around me seemed fazed in the slightest by that paradox. And regardless of my confusion, I was told to share this God with others: to make sure friends and relatives and classmates and strangers openly accepted His limitless love—so that He didn't pulverize them or put a pox on their houses (whatever that was).[1] I needed to rescue people from eternal torment before God came again to judge me and all of mankind: a tall order for a first grader. Nearly a half century later, I'm still carrying the remnants of these ancient relics around with me.

As an adult, have you ever really thought about the conclusions you hold about those elemental questions about the character of God and how you acquired them? How you would specifically describe whoever or whatever you believe holds everything together? What this God thinks of you and wants for and from you? You probably should. Your ability to be loving to yourself and your neighbors is in many ways a product of these conclusions; they make up the *whats* and *whys* of your spirituality. Whether we derive the answers from a sacred text, from life experience, from our community, from religious tradition, or from some entirely unique recipe of each of these, these answers dictate our sense of identity and self-love, orient us in the world, and give us purpose; they provide a filter for understanding suffering and favorable circumstances (are we being cursed, tested, or blessed?); and they also determine how we wield our religion as we encounter other people. These answers form the working theology of our ordinary lives.

One set of answers will yield a hopeful, compassionate benevolence that continually moves us to welcome others in and to live with an openhanded generosity—and another is likely to construct a scalding, brimstone-laden judgmentalism that leaves us predisposed to exclude and prone to finger wagging. (We all surely reside somewhere well between these two opposite poles.) Punitive religion, the kind many of us have been raised in and likely live in close proximity to, often preaches a conditional good news–bad news gospel where things seem promising presently, but the massive cosmic shoe is perpetually about to drop. Yes, God loves us unquestionably and effusively (we are told), but there are caveats and conditions under which we earn and keep that love: prerequisites for belonging among God and God's people, the moral scores that need to be settled in order to be fully welcomed. It may be helpful to leave behind those scary stories of our childhoods because they make for terrified adults, and terrified adults historically do not love very well.

BEING AFRAID OF GOD

FEARING OTHERS AND MAKING OTHERS AFRAID

Ultimately, the greatest barrier in my recent journey to find a more compassionate God and to be a better reflection of that God in the world has been the familiar voice in my head that tells me that God is angry at me for no longer believing a story that now sounds fundamentally unloving to my ears or for pushing back against a Church that often seems antithetical to Jesus. I've had to lose much of my ol' time religion to find out that God had outgrown it, and things aren't as cut-and-dried as they once were. I suppose that's also the hazard of imagining a better God and rethinking what loving your neighbors really looks like: we run the risk of imagining ourselves right out of comfortable belief.

There's an epidemic of that internal turbulence right now, as a result of an *actual* epidemic. In the middle of March 2020, the coronavirus outbreak in America quickly blossomed from some distant footnote global news item into a screaming doorstep emergency as cases started to climb rapidly and the seriousness of the situation was becoming clear—and almost overnight everything changed. In a span of just twelve hours, Disney World closed, the NCAA basketball tournaments were canceled, all professional sports were postponed, national and international concert tours were halted, and travel from Europe ceased for thirty days (at the time). Church services were called off, schools shut down, and so many usual collective expressions of community were suddenly nonexistent. The normal rhythms of life had been interrupted for all of us and it was genuinely disorienting, like trying to feel secure in the middle of an earthquake: there was nothing stable left to stand on. The relentless changes and conflicting updates and news briefings were difficult to keep up with. You could see the tension spilling over into stores and parking lots, as people frantically scrambled to gather things like hand sanitizer, wet wipes, and toilet paper, which had all suddenly become worth more than gold on the online black market.

Growing up Christian, I remember reading about John the Baptist saying to his students and to those who would follow in the ways of compassion and mercy and love and justice: "Anyone who has two shirts should share with the one who has none, and anyone who has food should do the same."[2] I thought about that as I watched a frazzled woman with a shopping cart piled to overflowing with toilet paper, unwilling to give a single roll to another woman who was literally pleading with her for it. "This is the last package in the store, and we only need a few rolls," she said to the stranger. "Why don't we split the cost and share them?" The woman with the cart laughed and hurried away.

(Loving your neighbor as yourself apparently doesn't apply to the last precious pack of two-ply.)

Now, I won't assume the woman with the massive, teetering stockpile of Charmin was a professed follower of Jesus, but I imagine many supposed people of faith in America were similarly losing their practical religion in those moments and in the weeks and months that followed. Millions of human beings—who only a few days earlier would have preached a God of abundance and recited the Scriptures about people in the early Church who shared all their belongings[3]—were bodychecking strangers for wet wipes and preparing to auction vital organs on the dark web for a bottle of hand sanitizer. During the initial days of the crisis, lots of self-identified Jesus followers found their faith stretched to its limits, as they actually had to put their money where their prayers and songs have been. It's one thing to say you believe in loving your neighbor as yourself as you stand in a building on a Sunday when all feels well with your soul—and another completely when you're panic-stricken in the middle of a crowded big-box store, face-to-face with your desperate neighbor who doesn't want their kids to have to wipe themselves with dried leaves and cocktail napkins. It's easy to stand with outstretched arms and blissfully sing, "It is well with my soul," but far more challenging to see your 401(k) evaporating, your calendar being shredded in real time, and your pantry emptying—and to not have your voice shake. Terrorizing moments tend to reveal your actual religion as opposed to your declared one. That's when the *real* you shows up, and when the God you truly believe in is present and accurately revealed. Times of crisis are also when you find out how much you love your neighbor, how unloving your neighbors can be, and how close we all are to desperation. Now, I always keep toilet paper in my car, just in case.

But without a global pandemic to drive them to the surface, I see lots of terrified Christians in America every day, making a showy display of piety that masks how terrified they actually are. These frightened faithful have a profound and fundamental spiritual problem: their God is simply too small. Though their words speak of an immeasurable Maker with a limitless love, in reality they worship a deity made in their own image: white, American, Republican, male—and perpetually terrified of Muslims, immigrants, science, gay children, special counsel reports, mandalas, Harry Potter, Starbucks holiday cups, yoga, wind turbines—everything. While they declare this God's staggering might at every opportunity, their defensive posture belies this confidence. They seem to feel the need to be armed to the teeth and to build impenetrable walls for protection, certain that others mean them harm and want to take what is theirs. They want to change gay couples and transgender teenagers themselves, because they don't trust God to work within people as God desires. They seem burdened to hoard wealth, health insurance, and opportunity—because they subconsciously suspect the God they claim turned water into wine and fed thousands with a few fish and some leftover bread might not make enough for everyone. They're worried about other religious traditions having a voice, lest their one, true God be offended by people worshiping in different ways.

I don't assume these Christians are any less authentic or less faithful than I am. I know they believe in God earnestly, pray to God passionately, and serve God with unflinching fervor. The problem is that their God is too small, and as long as they are oriented toward such a tiny, overmatched deity, they will continue to have a religion that is marked by fear more than by love, and that is simply no good for anyone. I feel sorry for them and for the world that has to be subjected to their pocket-size theology when there is an expansive space waiting for them. I hope and pray that these people soon find a God who is big enough so that they stop living so small, for their sake and for ours. People deserve a God who so loves the world, not a God who chooses America First; whose creation begins without divides and borders and walls, because there is only a single, interdependent community. People deserve a God who touched the leper and healed the sick and fed the starving and parted the seas and raised the dead—not a quivering idol who builds walls and drafts bathroom bills and launches social media crusades against migrant families. People deserve a God who is neither white nor male nor cisgender, nor heterosexual nor Republican—because any other God isn't big enough to bear the title or merit any reverence.

Ever since the pandemic alarms were first sounded by health officials, two scenes played out over and over on my social media timeline: photos and videos of barren grocery store shelves, and of massive, snaking lines of visibly shaken people pushing shopping carts filled to overflowing. As I saw the lack of supply and the panic of the demand commingling, I couldn't help but think of Jesus' instruction to his followers to pray for their "daily bread": not bread for a month or a year but for a single day, for the meal needed in this moment.[4] Granted, he might have said it differently back then, had his hearers had double-door refrigerators and an overflow chest freezer in the garage—but the bedrock of that prayer is the assurance of sustenance, of provision, of enough. It is a prayer of petition, only for what is necessary to weather the present, which isn't how we like to live when in crisis. In those moments we want to get as much bread as we can.

It's tempting to get ahead of ourselves when adversity visits. If we're being honest, on our very best days a terrifying sense of scarcity is always hovering in the periphery of our minds, and we're always struggling to keep it at bay,

TRUSTING IN GOD'S ABUNDANCE

FREEDOM TO BE GENEROUS

continually trying to discard the weights of the *what-ifs*. We're worried we won't have enough in the cupboards, that the money will run out, that we will lose ground, that we will be left without—even if privilege and prosperity shield many of us from all but a remote possibility of many of these things actually coming to pass. Yes, we want to boldly declare that *God provides,* but we also want to hoard enough

stuff to hold us for a few months just in case God doesn't—even if we have to build bigger barns[5] or rent storage spaces or throw away perfectly good stuff to accommodate it all. In the tenth chapter of Matthew's biography of Jesus, the writer records his teacher reminding those listening who are prone to worry that if God attends to the sparrows (who are worth half a penny on the open market), we can be sure that we too are in great care, given our special resemblance to Divinity.[6] This declaration isn't easily adopted when panic has seized us and the waters of anxiety rise swiftly around us. In those moments (like the ones the world is waking to on most days lately), it's telling where we'll look for security: a toilet paper surplus, a stockpile of bread, a bottled water cache—and maybe a loaded arsenal to guard it all. Paradoxically, many of those rushing to panic-buy toiletries and fill a second freezer are the same people simultaneously making a public stand of showy religion and loudly claiming to trust God to keep them safe from this virus and refusing to wear a mask. They have a selective sustenance that leans on faith or claims compassion until those things bring discomfort or involve too much sacrifice. While some professed believers abandon safeguards in the name of faith, others see wearing a mask and social distancing in a pandemic as a profoundly spiritual act, one that respects the gift of the knowledge of how viruses travel, and embodies loving their neighbor as themselves because they believe the God who made everything also resides in them. Theology is fully unmasked in crisis.

In some ways, the kind of isolation and restriction we've been living with during the virus outbreak has done something incredibly useful. It's renovated our collective religion by separating us geographically, taking away many of the familiar aspects of our communal spiritual existence, the superficial trappings and superfluous elements attached to the buildings we make weekly Sunday pilgrimages to. With those ultimately nonstructural parts of our belief systems stripped away, what's left are the foundation and the "bones" of what we really trust is holding this all together— which may or may not be very much. Fear is helpful. It's clarifying. It's illuminating. Whether or not we claim a religious worldview at all, fear burns up what we *say* we believe and reveals what we *actually* believe about protection, sustenance, security, generosity, abundance, and community. Fear shouts our convictions with bullhorn force: all the pretense falls away and the veneers crumble and the costumes dissolve and people see us as we really are.

Fear—the unprecedented, scalding, paralyzing kind we've all been immersed in during the pandemic—is also a beautiful invitation to step into the swirling chaos and be the best kind of humans we're capable of being, the people of light we aspire to be, the redemptive community the songs declare we are, the Church we imagine in our heads, a loving emulation of the God we claim faith in. When scarcity makes selfishness rise up, we can eclipse it with generosity. When separation feels safer, we can lean harder into risky community. When conspiracy and untruth come to stoke the fires of panic, we can bring the cool water of fact and truth. When our knee-jerk response is to hoard for *our own,* we can remember that we are in this together, that we are our brother's keeper, that we all belong to one another. When people around us are battered by the turbulence of uncertainty, we can steady them with our quiet, sober presence. If we pay attention, terrifying crises can remind us of our commonalities, of the fears and worries that assail all of us, regardless of the buffers we have or try to put in place: fears of not having enough or losing everything or dying alone. Days like these can remind us of our oneness—that

LETTING GO OF FEAR

REALIZING THERE IS ENOUGH

we are a single, interdependent community that transcends national borders, political affiliation, religious tradition, sexual orientation, nation of origin, or any delineation we see or create between people. That's what love demands of us.

Though I'm still trying to kick it, fear is one helluva drug. As far down the road as I travel from my old pathology, as small in the rearview mirror as I imagine my former orthodoxy is, and as many years out from my original deconstruction as I am, that snarling monster is still hovering in the shadowed periphery of my thoughts: the assurance that

I will get it wrong, piss off God, and bear the full weight of His fury. That toxin is never fully flushed from my system no matter how progressive I believe I am or how much I've tried to embrace my belovedness. It is an internal, portable relic of my former faith that occasionally addles me, and I know that misery is in good company. I understand the lady with the overflowing shopping cart well because I have the same debilitating impulses to hoard blessings, because I too worry that I won't have enough, and because once in a while I feel what it is to loosen my grip and find that sacred place called *enough.* That's why I wish she would have found enough compassion to give two rolls from her mega pack to her neighbor in need—because the act would have helped both of them. It would have lessened the burden for the stranger and allowed her to remember that better self she has access to—that we all have access to. And God, who works in the most mysterious of ways, would have shown up unceremoniously in the bath tissue section.

Though even the most untenable, terrifying times likely won't destroy us physically, they will surely define us morally: in grocery store aisles and our neighborhoods and online and in our living rooms. That's where our faith and our religion and our God show themselves. Perfect love is supposed to cast out all fear,[7] but fear doesn't leave easily. We're going to have to have the courage to stay and fight for people.

Chapter 3
THE SH*T IS NEVER GETTING TOGETHER

God, I cannot get my sh*t together.

That's probably what the title of this book should be (though I'm guessing that may not stick, for obvious reasons). However, if my spiritual journey over the past half century could be honestly summarized in a sentence, I can think of few better for the task. As a twenty-seven-year pastor, I've spent decades trying to convince other people that I'm absolutely certain of everything in matters of belief while not being completely sure of much of anything. In the quiet moments, far away from the flattering spotlights of megachurch pulpits, conference platforms, and viral blog posts, I've lived with the persistent voice that says, "You know you don't know what the hell you're doing, right?" (Maybe you recognize that voice?) I used to think that was *The Enemy* trying to deceive me (a convenient defense mechanism built into my default Christian story for any unpleasant experiences or uncomfortable moments) but now I realize it wasn't a lurking devil but an honest friend, keeping me grounded enough to remember that you don't become an expert in divinity as a human being, any more than you become an authority on the afterlife while you're alive. As terrifying as it is both personally and vocationally and as much as it makes some people (including myself) uneasy, little by little I'm finally settling into a humility that can admit this vast, continual learning curve. I'm growing more comfortable with all that I don't know; with the incomplete thoughts and the unresolved conflicts and the uncomfortable silences of trying to connect with a creator who seems reclusive on some days and downright antagonistic on others.

I suppose this infinite expanse of uncertainty is as good a place as any to start. It's where all authentic spiritual journeys begin: the cavernous gap between the need and the knowing, that messy, not-yet space of wanting more information than you have about the most pressing questions of this life.

You and I are always there (along with every other human being who's ever made their home on this planet),

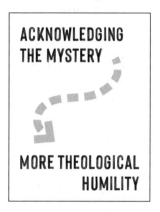

ACKNOWLEDGING THE MYSTERY

MORE THEOLOGICAL HUMILITY

and it's a really freeing thing when you realize the commonality in our shared struggle regardless of our faith tradition or religious worldview. Despite our pedigree or profession or our claims of *blessed assurance,* none of us really knows what we're doing here. You and I and Mother Teresa and Franklin Graham and the guy on the corner with a bullhorn condemning random pedestrians and the awkward high school student handing you your value meal—we are all working with incomplete information on the infinite, and we could all use a little kindness and a bit of mercy. There is a necessary level of mystery that spirituality cannot exist without (one the psalmist seemed aware of and perfectly comfortable with),[1] and the net effect of that mystery is that you and I are always going to be wondering about something, as long as we're being honest with ourselves. Whether we're overconfident zealots or hedging agnostics, whether we feel totally right with God or like heretics certain to be sentenced to eternal teeth-gnashing, whether we never utter a blue word or cuss with great creativity, it's comforting to know that the difference between the saved and the damned may just be a matter of what story we choose to believe—whether we are prone to guilt or grace toward ourselves when we fail and toward other people when they don't meet our standards or match our conclusions.

That's why a working theology of love matters so much: when we lead with gentleness, it decreases the chances that we will bulldoze someone with self-righteousness, because we honestly believe that we're no better than they are and no greater authority on anything. I think all intellectually honest religious people should suffer from some level of impostor syndrome, as if they don't quite have a handle on things, as if they are a hair's breadth from collapse. That kind of humility keeps you open to slightly revising or even totally dismantling your theological framework when experience begins to push against it. It makes you softer toward other stumbling pilgrims on the journey because you feel kinship with them in their struggles. In my experience, the confessed failures and admitted frauds are far more benevolent than the self-anointed angels and the saints are, anyway. People aware of their deficiencies are always more loving than those who are oblivious to them, even if they're an endangered species these days.

As I write this, I'm sitting in a small indie coffee shop adjacent to a Southern Baptist seminary (which, honestly, usually makes me feel like a rebel soldier tiptoeing carefully around inside the Death Star with stolen blueprints

for the Resistance). I'm surrounded by clusters of gloriously bearded young men discussing hermeneutics, moms
with careening toddlers in tow engaged in a women's Bible
study curriculum, and a table of khaki-wearing (and noticeably, exclusively male) professors talking about "taking the
gospel to the global mission field"—and I am eavesdrop-
ping at Olympic levels and writing furiously while trying
not to be noticed. They all seem like (and I'm quite certain
are) decent, thoughtful, earnest people, and surely far more
complex to me here than if I encountered them on my social
media timeline, where I might be tempted to reduce them to
convenient cookie-cutter stereotypes trapped in a dismis-
sive partisan meme. As I lean into the cacophony of their
colliding conversations to try to isolate and record them all
in real time, I'm struck by their common overconfidence:
the real (or assumed) subtle bravado that undergirds their
exchanges, how seemingly self-assured they all are as they
discuss and postulate and sermonize about the unfathomable mysteries of life and afterlife as if they're discussing
making a BLT. There is a *matter-of-factness* that sounds
impossible to me now, given the subject matter, but it's one
I'm well versed in as a longtime pastor. On this day, I'm not
sure whether to be angered or insecure about how certain
they are—so maybe I'll settle for being a bit of both.

In many ways, this coffee shop is a microcosm of what
organized Christianity looks like to many outside of it—and
indicative of what spiritual community can often slip into
if we build it on the image of unwavering surety: a cult of
sanctified sameness, devoid of the deviation that naturally
comes with free will and truly disparate company. Whatever
our theological or political leanings, our echo chambers of
affinity often allow us a safe space to reinforce our rightness
and shield ourselves from too invasive an interrogation—but

they usually don't invite the turbulence they should, the kind Jesus regularly hosted as he gathered with the religious elite and the godless street rabble. We usually confine our community to one side of the aisle or one side of the tracks, so to speak, editing out those voices most divergent from our own. As diverse as we aspire to be in churches, in reality we're probably a lot more homogenous than is healthy. Sure, we may occasionally get a tiny bit of gentle pushback from largely like-minded people, but nothing that makes us uncomfortable enough to cause real introspection or to generate a genuine doctrinal pivot— and certainly nothing that's going to stroll in and violently turn over the entire table on us.

HAVING A DIVERSE COMMUNITY

HEALTHY STRETCHING OF IDEAS

Surety is a nice idea, but it's highly overrated. There's a dangerous hubris involved in claiming any kind of moral authority or precise theological clarity other than "Here's the best guess I can make based on the available information— though I very well may be wrong." (I'd love more Sunday sermons like that, and I think most church people would too.) That's all we can really offer one another anyway, whether we're willing to admit it or not: our suspicions in this moment, knowing we'll likely feel differently tomorrow. What some people call moral inconsistency, I call personal growth. We see that in the Bible, in people like Moses and the apostle Paul, who in different ways became traitors to their old tribes and heretics to their former selves. I take great joy in arguing with who I was yesterday because I know twenty-four hours more about living than that guy did. Maybe that's what it means to pray for your "daily bread": sustenance in the present and fuel to propel us into the coming day, when we'll have a little bit more life to draw from and a whole new set of questions. For two decades as a "professional Christian," my work and livelihood were invested in the illusion of *knowing God stuff,* in having ironclad answers at the ready in matters of the greatest consequence. People would (and still do) come to me carrying their muddied thoughts, persistent questions, and nagging terrors, expecting me to bring some clarity that had escaped them—and for a while I did my best to embrace the myth that I could. It took me a long time to realize that wasn't good for either of us. I've slowly outgrown my sanctified surety, semiretired from being a theological know-it-all, and said farewell to some beliefs that once seemed impossibly permanent.

If you've evolved or matured or progressed in some fundamental way, you know that there's a grieving in that growing and outgrowing, in losing some of the old story, the security of that story, the sense of self that story gave you, and sometimes, even the characters from that story. As you stretch to become a more loving human or faith community, there will be losses along the way, people who will find your expanding perspective uncomfortable. That's an occupational hazard of being a human or a community trying to grow and to love better.

I can remember talking with a Missouri pastor in the wake of the 2016 election about reticence in her church and among its leadership to publicly step into the fray of social justice issues, for fear of upsetting their more conservative white members. When she complained that their collective silence was doing more damage to already oppressed and vulnerable people by yielding to the sensitivity of the most privileged people in their community, one of her long-tenured members said, "But pastor, we *want* these conservative members to come with us where we are going." The pastor agreed with this man in principle, but replied, "Maybe we have to really *go* there first and realize that not everyone will come with us. Maybe we have to be willing to lose some people in order to become the community we're supposed to become for those who aren't even here yet." As the church slowly stepped into that place of clarity and specificity around current social issues and more visible involvement in the work of justice, some longtime members indeed walked away, but many stayed and were joined by an entirely new group of gifted, passionate human beings who'd have never found a spiritual home in its former iteration. The pastor later said to me, "If we had refused change in order to placate people who weren't all-in with us, we'd have missed the chance to really be present in our city in the way we are now." For her, the discomfort and the grieving have been worth it, because those additions and subtractions have been a necessary part of their transformation. They needed that painful relational shifting to take place in order to become what they needed to become—and maybe you do too.

I wonder what you've lost on your way to becoming who you are. I wonder what separations and subtractions have resulted from your efforts to better love people. More than that, I wonder what you're willing to endure and let go of and part with as you move forward, in order to become who you need to become. I've endured firings, disconnections, ghosting, angry emails, and public insults along the path to a religion that felt more authentic. I've had to be OK with outgrowing organized religion and feeling the odd

homelessness that comes when one does. You likely understand some of that displacement: being a prodigal from the
homeland of your earlier faith story, sensing you don't quite
fit in the old spaces, suspecting you probably can't go back
even if you wanted to.

Yesterday, I shared a post empathizing with people
who often find Christians to be the most hypocritical and
unloving people on the planet, to which an old friend
replied, "So, what *are* you now?" I know she expected a better answer than the one I gave her: "It depends on the hour.
I'll let you know for sure in another fifty-one years." Some
days it's difficult to know *what* I believe about God anymore,
how much of my childhood religion I still hold firmly to with
mature hands, just what kind of faith I can fully claim today
with any conviction. When your faith begins to shift, it can
be daunting to know how much of your current belief system is a rejection of the old one. Often, I need to cut through
the strangling overgrowth of the story I tell myself in order to
unearth what's really there. I have to face my fraudulence and
inconsistency and hypocrisy, as I dislocate a hip[2] wrestling
the tag team of both the God I used to believe in and the One
I want to believe in. When I do, I realize that there are fleet-
ing moments when it all makes sense (or at least when I'm at
peace with the senselessness), when all the dots don't need
to connect, when I don't feel compelled to reconcile every
discrepancy, when I'm perfectly comfortable hovering somewhere between orthodoxy and heresy. Here, far from organized religion in this decidedly disorganized spirituality, the
assurance of things unseen that I'd always read about isn't
so much confirmed in my head as it is housed in my gut; it's
more emotional awareness than intellectual decision. I can't
quantify it, but its presence is undeniable. Along the journey
to a more authentic spirituality and a more loving expression

of it, I've had to hold more loosely a label I'd found a good deal of my identity in: *Christian*. Right now, my best answer to the question of "What *am* I?" is that I am someone trying to follow that internal burden to its source, wherever that leads. I am an *asker* with more questions, a *seeker* still looking, a *knocker* approaching new doors. That's a pretty good space to occupy.

GROWING SPIRITUALLY

GRIEVING YOUR OLD STORY

Today I drove behind a truck with a bumper sticker that asked, "How's my driving?" followed by a phone number. I wanted to call the number and simply say, "Lousy," and hang up—then realized that not only was this not a Christian response, but they probably had caller ID. I bet the person behind the wheel considers themselves a good driver. Most of us do, which explains why there are 17,250 car accidents per day in America.[3] (Just imagine if we were all bad drivers.) Lately, I'm not as concerned with defining for people *what* I am, as I am in asking them *how* I am: What do they think I believe based on the things I do and the causes I support and the way I treat people? If I never professed my spiritual beliefs, what would they imagine those beliefs were? Could they reverse engineer my theology? Right now, those of us who believe in a God who is love are going to have to do much better at convincing people that we believe that, before we'll ever expect them to. Maybe you should ask someone around you how your "driving" is—and really listen.

I don't think there's such a thing as a religious expert, which is why I'm usually uneasy whenever I hear people elevate anyone to this position. I don't care how many books you've read, how many years you devote to study, the number of letters you have following your name, how eloquent an orator you are, how well you string together written words, or how revered you are in theological circles—the fact of the matter is that none of these things provide certainty regarding the *hows* and *whys* of this life. In fact, if you're moving with honesty in this journey of meaning, you don't end up knowing more along the way, you simply learn how little you've understood to this point, how much you've gotten wrong in the past, and you grow more reverent and aware of the wonder just beyond the measurable things. You consent to the mystery and you admit the incompletes—which isn't easy to do when organized religion teaches you from birth that God is perfectly knowable and tells you it will make the personal introduction that only it can. Religion tends to try to cram the infinite not only into a box, and not only into our particular tradition's box, but into our preferred version of that box. For so many of us, the need to be right slowly indoctrinates us into a cozy cult of confirmation bias that reinforces what we already believe instead of daring us to believe something that might be more challenging yet more fully true.

People rarely look back on their past theology and think, "I wish I'd been more intolerant." They almost always regret not being more open to the possibility that they have something to learn. They almost always realize they didn't know as much as they thought they did. Stay teachable and you'll be more able to stay loving.

Someone once said to me, "John, faith is a funny thing. If you talk out loud to no one when you're in a church, they call you *faithful*. If you do it on a park bench or a bus, they call you *crazy*." I've often wondered about that eggshell-thin line between faithful and crazy, between having a personal relationship with someone I love whom I can't see or hear or touch, and with being not quite well. Depending on the day and the time, I can feel either description fits. Is it some soothing cocktail of fear, self-delusion, and desperation causing me to interpret feelings, events, and circumstances as confirmation of someone communicating with me without any quantifiable evidence—or is it that universe-birthing Love that holds us all, making itself small and quiet enough so that I have to lean in and linger long enough to hear it? That's the paradox of a right-sized God: God must be big enough to speak creation into being and set time into motion, and yet personal enough to know why those words of criticism I heard one day when I was five years old still make me feel insecure at fifty-one. God is architect of both the Milky Way and my heart. That's a lot to ask and even more to make much sense of. If there's any constant in the search for this God, it should be marked by unsettledness, like trying to wrap your arms around fog.

This whole spirituality endeavor is an exercise in grabbing hold of intangible things, so it's bound to be a disorienting mess if we're doing it right and coming clean with ourselves and with one another along the way. I respect people who approach belief intellectually, people who want evidence and who seek an informed religious worldview based on measurable, tangible data—but I also know that the New Testament scribe was right when he said that faith isn't about surety but about suspicions;[4] it is an aspirational orientation, a movement toward something just slightly out of reach, something that propels you to ask and seek and knock—because you don't know it all yet. There is nothing organized or neat or easy about this, so we should all invite the chaos in, make friends with it, learn to live with it, and see the imperfect process of coexisting with it as a holy act itself. In the Gospel stories, it wasn't just listening to the Sermon on the Mount[5] preached on a hillside that altered Jesus' disciples, it was the sea-soaked terror in the back of the boat,[6] it was pressing their toes into the cool, rich soil of the vineyard, and in fully grieving around the grave of their beloved friend. It was in their doubts and their competitive sparring and their unthinkable hillside meals alongside multitudes that they found proximity with the bigger thing—and even then, they couldn't quite make sense of everything. When it comes to knowing all the mysteries while we're here, the sh*t is never getting fully together, so we should manufacture a little grace for other people and for ourselves—and love everyone well in the mess.

Chapter 4

THOU SHALT NOT BE A JERK

I'm a jerk and so are you. Not always, of course, but sometimes, and that *sometimes* is what we want to pay close attention to if a loving expression of our personal and collective
spirituality really matters to us and if we're truly burdened
to alleviate the damage in the world and not contribute to
it. In order to better do that, it might be helpful to define
our terms before going any further and answer the elemental question, *So, what's a jerk, anyway?* This may not be as
simple as we imagine.

In 1964, in a case deciding the nature of pornogra-
phy, Supreme Court Justice Potter Stewart remarked that
although defining obscenity was a challenge, recognizing it
was not. He famously declared (with unintended hilarity),
"I know it when I see it."[1] When it comes to the jerks in
our lives, we can usually spot them without much difficulty
as well, even if specifying their defining qualities proves
tricky—and with a little thoughtful reflection or sincere
prayer, we can surely recognize the *jerkiness* in ourselves.
Sit back and review the day you've had today, for example,
and I bet you can recognize it without much effort. You
know when either on social media or at home or at your job,
you've set out to hurt another human being and succeeded.
Congratulations, you've been a jerk.

Generally speaking, it isn't necessarily our particular theological worldview, political perspective, or personal opinion that is problematic, but the manner in which we wield them and our purpose for wielding them the way that we do. It isn't always the message; sometimes it's the heart of the messenger. We often imagine that being a loving person means never causing injury or initiating conflict, but it's more complicated and subtle than that. In this life, you've surely hurt other people, and you've done so in one of two ways: either you've accidentally injured someone by saying or doing something that you weren't aware was offensive or painful to them—or you've intentionally wounded them because that was either partially or fully what you were trying to do from the beginning. In the former case you were *human,* and in the latter case you were a *jerk*—and often-

PUTTING THEOLOGY OVER PEOPLE

HURTING PEOPLE IN GOD'S NAME

times you're the only one who knows the truth. The first instance requires self-awareness and honesty to repair the damage, while the second necessitates repentance and a severe attitude adjustment, and that's a much taller order.

All that to say that as we incarnate our belief systems and make the theoretical tangible, motives matter. In relationships with other people, we will cause inadvertent pain through ineloquence, privilege, carelessness, haste, or arrogance—and those wounds can't be dismissed and need to be reckoned with. (We can't just ignore the collateral damage of our words and actions simply because we didn't mean to hurt someone or didn't know any better.) But there *is* something far more toxic in desiring to inflict trauma, especially if we do so while simultaneously claiming moral high ground or righteousness in the process.

People regularly show up in my in-box or on my timeline or in my comment section because something I've written or said has caused them . . . extreme discomfort. They often arrive announced and unceremoniously unload a fierce and brutal verbal assault in protest or dissension often peppered with vitriol, punctuated with profanity, and littered with expletives. That's not to say these replies don't sometimes include valid criticisms, but the packaging can certainly be less than pleasant. In those moments and in the conversations that flow from them I have to continually ask myself, *Am I trying to understand this person, or am I trying to defeat them? Am I burdened to show them something I've seen or experienced that they haven't or to show them how much smarter or more enlightened I am? Am I genuinely seeking to change their hearts—or am I trying to make them feel like an a-hole?* I know which answers my faith demands of me, the path Jesus carved out for me. I also know how addictive the alternative can be, the cheap temporary high of putting someone on blast or verbally dismantling them. I bet you do too. We all understand how intoxicating winning an argument or making someone feel stupid can be— but we also know that's not what love does, don't we? We almost always look back retrospectively and can see where we've blown it and where we got it right.

That isn't to say that just because we get it right that people will respond well to us. Jesus wasn't always received with open arms and appreciative hearts, so we can't expect to be. We need to remember that there is no inherent evil in acknowledging difference or naming opposing views, but there may be if your disagreement is marked by extreme prejudice or premeditated cruelty. Jesus' command to love our neighbors and our enemies does not come with guarantees that we won't offend or bring discomfort or create turbulence (as sometimes love surely does those very things), but Jesus *is* telling us to keep our hearts as blameless as we can while we do. He is commanding us to seek our better angels in the trenches of relational disconnect by making every effort not to harm. He is cautioning us against being cruel in his name, partly because of the way we ourselves are transformed as we lean into compassion, and partly because most people are already pretty beat up and could use a little kindness.

My son and I are avid Philadelphia Eagles fans (a very *different* religion, the euphoric highs and expletive-laden lows of which merit another book altogether). As the kickoff of 2020's strange, fanless, pandemic-altered season approached, our team had already somehow been decimated by a litany of training-camp injuries that left us feeling dejected well before the first game even began (a default setting for the perpetually perturbed Philly faithful). In the national pregame show, a local beat writer reporting from the nearly empty stadium read the names of all the nearly dozen players confirmed to be out for the approaching contest, but said of one of the most critical of them, "He's playing hurt but he'll be playing." We were relieved, but we also knew this player's dubious medical status didn't bode well for our chances. *Playing hurt* essentially means someone is physically compromised, in considerable pain, certainly not at full capacity—but is showing up anyway and contributing to the team as much as possible despite their various limitations.

The phrase resonated loudly with me on this particular Sunday, because I too was playing hurt. It was my father's birthday and the seventh anniversary of his sudden passing while on a Caribbean cruise, and I was having a painful out-of-body experience. Even though I was physically there in our living room laughing and helping my kids dispatch a glorious, glistening tower of transcendent buffalo wings, had earlier delivered a rousing virtual message on staying hopeful for a local church, and was later going to host an online conversation with some local activists about the upcoming election—I wasn't at my best by a long shot. For most of the morning, I'd been continually fighting back tears, struggling to concentrate, and feeling far less than at full strength, though I took comfort in knowing I was in good, grieving company.

Two days prior, America had paused en masse to remember the nearly three thousand people who died in the 9/11 terrorist attacks of 2001, and anyone old enough to remember the abject horror of that day was surely carrying the heaviness around with them in silence, the still seemingly fresh images and the emotions that simply defy description. And they were doing it all in the middle of an already gut-punching year absolutely upended by a relentless pandemic, explosive civil rights protests, and the most divisive election season of our lifetimes (and their own specific set of personal challenges on top of it all). On that day of collective sadness, they too had obligations and deadlines and responsibilities that didn't disappear simply because they'd rather have fully devoted themselves to grieving. They too had to go about the necessary work of living with a lingering sadness residing just below the surface. So, they suited up and participated while nursing injury. They did the laundry and processed paperwork and made dinner and fixed the kids' bikes, and they limped and winced all the while because that's what good humans do in bad times.

That's always the case, which is why as people of faith, morality, and conscience we're lucky to be here on such fertile holy ground right now. As jacked up as the world is, we get to be the people who show up and remind it that goodness still inhabits this place, that loving human beings haven't called it a day—and that's a pretty easy thing to forget. Even without 2020's exacerbating issues of a global health crisis or any national tragic anniversary to alter us emotionally, it would still be true that everyone around you is *playing hurt* in some way: all nursing hidden wounds, all living with chronic emotional pain, all carrying invisible burdens, and all doing their very best to show up even though they're at far less than full capacity—because someone is counting on them to be present and to make them feel seen and heard and valued.

That is the sacred space we're invited to step into, carrying with us whatever we feel we can bring, which is more

than we usually realize. I've always loved the story of Jesus feeding the multitude,[2] because the first thing he does before making the miraculous meal is ask his disciples, "What do you have? What can you come up with?" Now, he knows they aren't capable of providing everything required, but they *are* capable of providing *something:* something that he will multiply and magnify, a small gift that gets transformed as it leaves their hands. This is how we live spiritually in the middle of physical and emotional trauma: knowing that our meager, seemingly insufficient offerings change the situation, and they change us too. And the opposite is as true: when we sidestep the need around us, when we ignore the pain in our path (or worse, when we intend harm), we can make an already painful journey unbearable—not just in the moment, but for a lifetime.

Recently, a Grammy-nominated songwriter from Nashville named Terry asked if I'd be willing to answer some questions about a family issue, and we arranged a video chat later that day. Now in his late forties, he'd been raised in a fundamentalist church until his senior year in high school, when he was outed by his youth pastor and—in an example of unthinkable cruelty—was expelled from the community by a group of students and adult leaders after refusing to "publicly repent of the sin of his sexuality." All this time later, Terry fought back tears while telling me (a relative stranger) the story of the past two and a half decades: a scarred prodigal's jagged pilgrimage, repeatedly trying to find acceptance in a faith community that made him feel unwelcome, working tirelessly to be fully loved by a family who continually reminded him that they didn't approve of his lifestyle, and trying for almost thirty years to find his way back home to a God he's so long believed despised him but desperately hoped didn't. He said to me, "Every day of my life, Christians preached a Jesus they absolutely refused to show me. They were always 'love, love, love' but I received none of it, and so I walked away. Actually, I ran." He continued, "I'm not sure what I believe anymore about what happens after you die, but I know that if hell exists, it probably feels like what Christians have put me through for most of my life."

If you've been paying attention, you know Terry's not an exception. You know he is one of the thousands of walking wounded around you, whose most enduring spiritual obstacle is people who profess faith in a Jesus they seem to have little interest in obeying or imitating. Maybe you're among this weary multitude who believe that religion should leave people feeling more human, not less—or it's a bad use of time and a waste of fading daylight. If so, be encouraged: you and Jesus have a great deal in common. His exasperation with those who loudly declare a grace they seem determined not to extend to everyone shows up throughout the Gospels (see Matthew 15:1–8). He is continually dismantling people's well-curated facades of religiosity to determine what is holding them together underneath, forever measuring the space between what they say they believe and what their lives confirm they actually believe. To paraphrase Jesus speaking to a judgmental crowd of self-righteous hypocrites ready to pounce on a supposedly morally inferior adversary: "Let he who is without sin be an intolerable jerk."[3] In other words, we should be as gentle with others as God is with us, providing we can actually claim that gentleness for ourselves.

Singer Tom Petty once said, "If we're born in God's image, then God knows how we can f*ck up. And he knows that you really didn't mean it."[4] Now, if you were raised in a "proper Christian" home and endured the persistent ceremonial moral peer pressure of church community, you may be initially distracted by the profanity present in this quote or alarmed at what feels like certain heresy—but honestly, if God is love in its most complete and perfect form, and if that God is responsible for your and everyone else's existence, and if that God is intimately aware of the deepest contents of your heart—the immortal bard Petty has to be right, doesn't he? That *has* to be the most perfectly accurate sermon in the history of classic rock theology. If it isn't, we're all in big trouble here because it means that God has no idea how tough it is being human and what a challenge it is to believe and to live accordingly, given the continual learning curve and the degree of difficulty involved. I take great comfort in the fact that the bedrock of Jesus' teachings (in keeping with the great rabbinic tradition of holy curiosity) was inviting people to step into the questions: letting them share proximity with their unknowns and tensions, asking them to stop and consider their plank-eyed blind spots and untested assumptions of their belief system. He made people do the painful exploratory work of seeing into the depths of their own spirituality and confronting the gap between their testimony and their activity—to de-jerkify their lives. Just as it is right now, this often wasn't a pleasant experience, and people tended to avoid it at all costs.

We all have an aspirational theology, a best-case-scenario belief system that we'd like to have in a perfect world—and tend to imagine already exists. That's the steadfast faith and expansive love we glean from the songs and the prayers and the doctrinal statements. The problem is, we don't always embody that love as well as we'd like or assume we do—which means we are usually a lot less sure and kind than we tell ourselves we are. Not only that, but it might be our very theology that needs alteration in order to make us more loving. This may be encouraging or terrifying information, depending on how comfortable you are with existential crises and admitted fraudulence; just know that if you ever feel a nagging sense of hypocrisy or a persistent, hovering doubt, you're in good company. That's a biblical thing and God is OK with it, so you should be too. For example, for the apostle Paul to fully embrace the teachings and way of Jesus, he had to become a traitor to his former self, passionately advocating for the very movement he once believed deserving of persecution. As his understanding of the love of the God he served expanded, so did his expression of that love, breaking down barriers that would not have fallen without a bit of what he first imagined to be heresy. He ended up providing shelter for the very people he'd assailed before.

We rarely get to opt out of life when it's painful (and it quite often is), which is why people of faith whose religion is marked by love are so necessary—because we are situated on the front lines of human beings in crisis in the way that Jesus was, and we can be a similarly peacemaking presence or we can choose not to be. Like him, we can (and should) be the helpers and the healers, the ones who alleviate suffering and reduce despair, the people facilitating restoration and hastening wholeness, the better angels of this sometimes hellish place. We get to be the concerned Samaritan stopping to attend to the wounds so many others walk by.[5] We get to be the grieving disciples, still making room for an unexpected guest.[6] When we refuse to be that kind of compassionate understudy, when we preach a gospel of enmity or contribute to the world's suffering, or when we fail to embody empathy, we rob people of the chance to know a bigger God than the undersized facsimile they may have often encountered, we miss the opportunity to surprise them with kindness, and we forfeit the chance to make people feel their inherent belovedness, which is the absolute highest calling there is. Perhaps worst of all, we further damage human beings already playing hurt, sometimes irreparably—and we do it in God's name.

It doesn't matter how you label your religious affiliation/tradition or the building where you gather or the creed you recite or who gets the credit on your timeline. If it doesn't substantially or partially compel you to be more compassionate, more loving, more aware of people's pain, and more moved to alleviate it, it's probably not made of

God stuff and it's not going to matter to the vast majority of human beings you encounter, who consider religion to be at best superfluous and at worst, toxic. This is the biggest disconnect for people who've lost or thrown away their religion, or temporarily misplaced it: they can't reconcile hateful people peddling a God of love, and they refuse to be told they have to. They will not abide intolerance no matter whom the person perpetuating it is passing the buck to. They're your exhausted, frustrated neighbors demanding a little Golden Rule kindness from the people who claim that love matters to them. They might also be the people you feel the least inclined to love, the people whom you imagine you have nothing in common with, those you believe are your adversaries. Jesus is there, disguised as the least of these and as your enemies.

WILLINGNESS TO CHANGE

POSSIBILITY OF GROWTH

My meandering, five-decade pilgrimage as a theological mutt—from obedient Catholic altar boy to disenchanted teen to hopeful agnostic to defiant atheist to overconfident United Methodist megachurch pastor to deconstructing progressive to humanist Christian to whoever and whatever I am today—hasn't yielded much in the way of definitive statements. In fact, the single conclusion I've come to as a result of all my study and prayer and wrestling and preaching, the sole fixed truth I can hold on to, is that *faith shouldn't make you a jerk*. That's it. (If you've read this and nothing else, I'll be happy and trust that you'll figure out what that means for you.) For me, it means that your theology is only valid to the degree that your life is loving. Beyond that, your preaching and proselytizing are largely a waste of time to people, especially if they don't have a religious affiliation or share your worldview. If God *is* actually love, then there's no other acceptable alternative. Jesus is in your living room and on your timeline. He is the person you love dearly and the person you don't at all like. He is the one you believe you have everything in common with and the one you can find no connection to. For the love of God, don't be a jerk to him.

Chapter 5
THE DUDE ABIDES

He's got the whole world in His hands.
He's got the whole world in His hands.
He's got the whole world in His hands.
He's got the whole world in His hands.

I learned this song so long ago that I actually don't remember learning it. It seemingly came with my default operating system as the child of Catholic parents: a part of parochial school programs and summer camps and Sunday school lessons. On its face, the heart of the song is steadying and beautiful: everyone and everything and everywhere is OK, because God's got it covered. All of creation is safe, including you. In this spirit, it is as "big-God" and as love-embracing an idea as you can have—like, planet-holding massive. But there is an odd caveat embedded in the lyrics that I didn't recognize for decades: yes, God is glorious and wondrous, limitless in beauty, unfathomable in scale, beyond our collective comprehension—but also a dude.

God the Father. God the man. God, the *He of Hes*. Throughout my life, I was taught that God most certainly was *all* of those things, and it has taken half a lifetime to comprehend how toxic, how dangerous, and ultimately how limiting an idea that is—and to begin to have God renovated in my head. I can remember being ten years old and hearing the sitcom soliloquy from that esteemed biblical scholar, *All in the Family*'s Archie Bunker: "In the Bible it says, 'God made man in His own image.' He made women after, from a rib, a cheaper cut."[1] Writer Norman Lear was skewering the misogynistic theology for laughs, but the words spoke eloquently about the dangers inherent in imagining a Divinity who is decidedly male, first creating a man and then creating a woman out of that man; it not only justifies all sorts of sexism both inside and outside the Church, but it gives license to pervasive ignorance about the breadth of gender identity and sexual orientation that actually exists and the way God is beautifully reflected in that complexity. So much of the fear-fueled violence Christians have generated toward LGBTQ human beings for centuries comes from the restrictive story we've inherited about a Maker who wears pants.

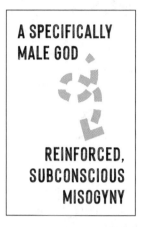

A SPECIFICALLY MALE GOD REINFORCED, SUBCONSCIOUS MISOGYNY

He loves us, oh how He loves us.
He loves us, oh how He loves us.[2]

Growing up, the idea of God as a white-bearded older gentleman was impossible to avoid. I lived for forty years with a decidedly male, Sistine Chapel God, and for most of that time it worked for me (as a white male, of course, it would). It seemed perfectly reasonable to accept the pronouns for the Almighty handed down by my parents and Sunday school leaders. I didn't even consider questioning it until I was old enough to realize that questioning it could get me in trouble (therefore, I stayed quiet). After all, the adults around me were just following the script drafted by the Old Testament writers, the disciples, and even Jesus himself. Sure, as I would begin to learn, there were numerous examples of feminine descriptions of God in the Bible,[3] but overall it definitely skewed masculine. The Gospels are conspicuously populated with numerous references by Jesus to his "Father in heaven," and the objects of many of his parables are decidedly male authority figures (king, master of the house, landowner, father).[4] This, in fact, became my last line of defense when people questioned the idea of a solely male deity or when I began to question it myself: *Well, Jesus did it—and if you can't trust Jesus as a Christian, well then, who can you trust?*

There are all sorts of factors that could explain the prevalence of a specifically gendered biblical God: translation issues from the original languages, cultural gender bias in the compilers and curators of the library of books that became the Bible, or perhaps Jesus' desire to make God approachable and relatable, using the kind of patriarchal figure people valued so highly at the time. Ultimately though, identifying the precise reasons *why* the Scriptures so often present a male creator are less important and manageable here than simply confronting the old assumptions, looking at them with fresh eyes, and asking: does a single-gendered God make any sense, and does it yield a more equitable world and a more loving religion? Does our inherited narrative of an old man running things, as comfortable or familiar as the image may be for some of us, pass the smell test? If we can imagine God outside the confines of gender, doesn't that unearth something more revelatory and wondrous? (If that question feels threatening or unsettling to you, might that be a *you* problem?) How can a God who is spirit and not body be accurately identified with qualifiers that we often associate with physicality: anatomy, physiology, and biology? If God does *not* have those markers to measure by (and it seems pretty clear God does not), just how exactly *can* that being/force/presence be identified as exclusively male? How did the writers of the Bible establish God's gender to begin with? If God is God, I'm not sure that God can be defined by or contained within a traditional gender definition—actually, I'm sure that's impossible. If all human beings are indeed made in the image of God, then God embodies and contains and transcends every current understanding we have of the complexity of gender.

That doesn't mean personifying God isn't useful for us. We exist in and engage this world relationally with other people, and we largely find our identity in the context of those relationships, so it makes sense that we all ascribe some personhood to the greater love that holds it all together. For those who've had a loving relationship with their fathers, it might be quite helpful to humanize God as father (especially because the muscle memory of our childhoods is so strong), but for just as many people, because of the toxic, abusive, or painful male relationships of their past, this becomes a liability, creating an inherently oppressive figure who perpetuates their previous mistreatment and magnifies their pain. This "male-pattern godness" also serves as a barrier for people outside of religion or those at the periphery of it, who look at a world moving toward a wider understanding of sexuality and a less patriarchal system, hear our man-centric language, notice our male-dominated churches, and immediately check out. For such people, imagining God as mother (also a biblical metaphor) or sister may be more fruitful; God as something, as *anything* but a guy, is actually great. If God is God-sized, that God can be father, maker, shepherd, mother,

guide, or friend. God has great range and can't be typecast—
and degendering God altogether might be really helpful if
we can manage it.

A Christian reader named Devin, incensed at my support
for transgender human beings, recently left this comment on my blog, one of many variations on this theme
echoed by others: "John, God knew what He was doing.
He created people either male *or* female. That old, gay talking point of gender fluidity is so tired."

Yes, that "old, tired, gay talking point," I replied,
"that one so many Christians can't stand—the one from
the Bible, which says *all* people are made in God's image."
The Genesis creation story (the one these folks cling fervently to and will defend to the death as literal and bind-
ing) quotes God as saying, "Let us make humankind in our
image, according to our likeness" (Genesis 1:26). Humans
are *all* made in the image of a God who defines *God's selves*
in the act of creation—in plurality. Some biblical scholars
contend this declaration of
God as "us" is actually a Trini-
tarian conversation (God, Son,
and Holy Spirit talking to one
another, for some unstated
reason). Others point to con-
straints in the translation from
Hebrew to Greek that demand
a plural pronoun (a sort of
royal "We"). But even if one
accepts one of these explana-
tions for the word used, there is still a question to answer:
Is the God of the Bible—maker of all humanity, the source

A GOD WHO
TRANSCENDS GENDER

THE ABILITY TO SEE
GOD IN EVERYONE

of all life equally—simply male or female? That seems like a huge disservice to the scale and scope of the Almighty. The only way every disparate human being could be equally and fully made in the likeness of God (if we're to use the same Bible these homophobic/transphobic Christians use) is if God both transcends and encompasses gender. If God is both male *and* female and neither male *nor* female, then this God (to quote my reader) is a tired "gay talking point."

The truth is, even though the Bible appears on the surface to reflect a limited and predominantly binary understanding of human sexuality befitting its ancient genesis, it uses images of and language for God that aren't strictly male:

> Can a woman forget her nursing child, or show no compassion for the child of her womb? Even these may forget, yet I will not forget you (God speaking in Isaiah 49:15).

> As a mother comforts her child, so will I comfort you; and you shall be comforted in Jerusalem (God speaking in Isaiah 66:13).

> But I have calmed and quieted myself, I am like a weaned child with its mother; like a weaned child I am content (David speaking of God in Psalm 131:2 NIV).

> Jerusalem, Jerusalem, you who kill the prophets and stone those sent to you, how often I have longed to gather your children together, as a hen gathers her chicks under her wings, and you were not willing (Jesus speaking in Matthew 23:37 NIV).

Ruach, the name for the Spirit of God in the original Old Testament Hebrew, is feminine. The femininity of God is everywhere.

A transgender God is as biblical as it gets. I know that for many Christians, these words feel confrontational, provocative—and quite blasphemous. If you are among them, that may be an alarm that you're hearing something you suspect rings true and is challenging the lens you've looked at God and other people through for your entire life. I get how terrifying such a deity gender identity crisis can be (especially if you're a man who always just assumed God is, too), but that discomfort and instability are worth facing, and the verses worth studying, and the idea worth entertaining—because ultimately, understanding God as merely a cisgender, heterosexual man shrinks God into something comfortable, something easily managed—and something far too small to be God. If we really believe God made every human being who has ever walked the planet, and that *each* of these people bears the DNA of their Creator, we're going to need to rethink the story we inherited. Maybe this whole gender identity and sexual orientation thing is a little more complex and expansive than we can glean from a 4,000-year-old poem (Genesis 1–2), and maybe we should stop using it to destroy other people. Maybe, rather than shrinking God any longer, we need to release God from that confining space inside our heads. And as difficult as it is, maybe we should expand our very image of God in a way that argues with our learned theology, because if we do, it might make us far more willing to treat the diverse humanity that crosses our paths with the reverence and respect each one of them deserves—as made by and of God.

Degendering or additionally gendering God as an idea can require a massive reboot for your brain, especially if you've spent a few decades with the righteous dude abiding there. If, like me, you have spent hundreds of hours in prayer circles, hearing people copiously peppering their petitions and praises with the phrase "Father God," you know how hard those habits are to break. As difficult as it may be for a Caucasian Christian to say good-bye to white Jesus, it is an equal challenge for many to bid farewell to a manly Maker, but it's important that we do, so that we can see the full spectrum of sexuality as equally sacred. God is decidedly nonbinary, and that is really good news, because it means that we can discover the character of that God in every human being we encounter without exception. It's intellectually dishonest to say that all human beings are image-bearers of the Divine and created in God's likeness—and yet insist that the Creator is a dude. God has to be gender-fluid, and that's a beautiful idea to settle into, because the scope and capacity of our love grows exponentially as a result. We become more liberal in our sharing of that love and less apt to withhold affection from anyone, because we recognize they are all fashioned by the same hands that we are. We don't need to believe that "He" has the whole world in "His" hands. We just need to trust that we are held.

Chapter 6
MADE IN AMERICA

Consider Matthew 22:35–39:

> [One of the religious leaders gathered] asked [Jesus] a question to test him: "Teacher, which commandment in the law is the greatest?"
>
> He said to him, "'You shall love the Lord your God with all your heart, and with all your soul, and with all your mind.' This is the greatest and first commandment. And a second is like it: 'You shall love your neighbor as yourself.'
>
> "But the third commandment trumps both of those," Jesus said. "You shall love America and make it great."

You won't find that third commandment in any of the dozens of English translations of the Bible currently available to you. You will, however, find it implicitly embedded in the theology of tens of millions of Christians you live, worship, study, and work alongside every day. Part of the default background operating system that's running churches and propelling political campaigns and directing hearts is the idea that God is American and the gospel was written down in red, white, and blue. If there's a single exegetical error most responsible for distorting the message of Jesus and for producing unloving disciples in the United States in the past 250 years, it's likely this. An America-centered religion is the singular genesis of the white supremacy, nationalism, xenophobia, and anti-immigrant rhetoric we're experiencing here. While certainly not created in November of 2016, this distorted theology has inarguably been in a prolific and creative renaissance ever since. In fact, if we remove the flag-waving, border-defending, proud-to-be-an-American firework fervor from many Christian people's belief systems, there's not much left, and that's a problem, because there are too many people who potentially exist outside the border of their empathy and the complexion of their care, too many ways this unmerited image of superiority can be exploited by the right person.

From the moment his presidential campaign began, Donald Trump promised to "Make America Great Again," and in the fall of 2016, 81 percent of white American evangelicals ended up passionately embracing both him and that message—and were largely responsible for his ascension to the presidency.[1] It seemed clear from his initial press conferences, his antagonistic tweets, and his incendiary rallies that the "greatness" Trump aspired to was going to be a country marked by vitriol, enmity, separation, bullying, wall building, and abject cruelty. It would be the construction of a heavily fortified gated community of frightened Caucasian believers, who he easily convinced were assailed on every side by a dangerous and diverse horde of quickly encroaching predators. In the past few years, this swift, grand march toward national "greatness" has been noticeably accompanied by a collective move away from goodness, by a hostility to outsiders and a startling lack of compassion for hurting and vulnerable people. This all underscores the painful truth: good wasn't part of the plan from the beginning. Sadder still, many of Trump's evangelical supporters have amened all this bitter, divisive malevolence while still simultaneously claiming Christ, blessing an effort to steamroll the world into greatness by force and coercion, and inexplicably contending that Jesus endorses it all.

The problem with all this is Jesus himself. He apparently had very little interest in such geographically determined supremacy or birthright blessings, or in the accumulated power that has proven to be such a seductive selling point to

EMBRACING AN "AMERICA FIRST" THEOLOGY

A GOSPEL THAT IS NOT FOR THE WHOLE WORLD

so many of his followers. He talked of the last being first, of becoming servant of all, of laying down one's life for one's friends. He affirmed the priceless values of denying oneself, of healing the hurting, of caring for the poor, of elevating the marginalized, of freeing the oppressed, of seeing the overlooked; of being peacemakers, foot washers, cheek turners, mercy givers. He wasn't in the business of nation building but community making, not about consolidating wealth but spreading it around and making sure no one went without. He was always doing the social justice work of raising valleys and leveling mountaintops. Jesus' life as witnessed in the Gospel stories was a beautifully subversive manifesto of smallness and kindness and goodness, continually reiterating the sacredness of sacrifice, the dignity of humility, the redemptive nature of forgiveness.

But these things don't make for effective campaign slogans or bright red hats, do they? They don't leverage the hidden fear in people's hearts or manufacture easy urgency from an ever-shrinking pool of Sunday pew sitters. Calls to selflessness don't induce lazy religious people into action by exploiting the image of a furious God dispensing damnation. They don't poke the tender places of anxiety and hatred, don't stoke the fires of latent racism and homophobia, and don't resonate when screamed from behind a podium. They don't fire up the anxious everyman and they don't appeal to the lowest common denominator. That's probably why Jesus claimed that the way of life-giving love was the very narrowest of roads, and why so few relatively affluent church people take it.

The character of Jesus doesn't rally the Bible Belt or garner the support of popular evangelists or fill glistening megachurches. Worst of all, it doesn't seem to seep into the souls of many professed Christians anymore either—which for a person of faith is the bigger story here: the growing irrelevance of Jesus in so much of the faith tradition that bears his name. This is the greatest sin of the American evangelical church in these days: normalizing, embracing, and celebrating the very kind of bloated, callous, parochial self-centered existence that Jesus came to call people away from—and it makes for a tragically ironic religion in which people boldly proclaim an upside-down gospel of privilege and supremacy that bears no resemblance to the good news for the poor and marginalized that Jesus claimed as his mission statement. The Christians most loudly preaching the greatness of America are abandoning the goodness of Jesus Christ, rightly driving decent people out of organized religion and then blaming them for leaving—instead of offering them hospitality and inviting them into something worth moving toward. The times they may be a-changin' but not all the Jesus people got the memo.

What we witnessed throughout America following the May 2020 murder of George Floyd was somewhat heartening because for the first time in a long time it drew a disparate response that cut across any delineations of political affiliation, religious tradition, or socioeconomic level—including many followers of Jesus, along all points of the theological spectrum. So many people who'd previously relegated themselves to the sidelines entered into the fray, and the numbers and the fervor of protesters tangibly moved the court of public opinion, sending ripples into all segments of the culture—including the NFL, which for four years had actively resisted Colin Kaepernick's silent, peaceful attempts to bring attention to the issues of systemic racism and police brutality like that exemplified in Floyd's death. Somehow, this moment proved catalytic when so many others had passed from public conversation with little more than a few hours of hashtagged social media posts tossed like bottle rockets. However, the collective moral outrage that points to a greater community of compassion forming has been tempered by the reality that the most passionate objection to this war on brutality and racial injustice was and is still coming largely from white Christians.

It's never lost on me that the greatest resistance to the Black Lives Matter movement and to LGBTQ equality and to so many other human rights movements comes from followers of Jesus. They are, in many cases, the loudest and most conspicuous holdouts. There are times when you realize how far the Church has drifted from the mission and how badly so many Christians have lost the plot—and it often comes when you see strange bedfellows gathering: agreement where there should not be agreement, affinities that should not exist, commonalities that defy logic.

One morning, while reflecting on the disheartening evangelical Christian support for Donald Trump's anti-immigrant rhetoric and proposed Muslim travel ban, I tweeted out these words: *Equality means believing that a child living 5,000 miles away is as precious as the one sleeping in your nursery right now.* I think that is what it means to imagine a God who *so loves the world,* to believe a Jesus who claimed he inhabits the bodies of the disregarded and the forgotten. Soon, my notifications were blowing up with angry replies from conservative Christians (which I'd gotten quite used to and barely registered) and, for some reason, from lots of Nazis as well (which tends to get one's attention). It took just a few moments of timeline investigation to realize that the tweet had been shared by alt-right suprema-cist hero Richard Spencer, whose black-boot-wearing fan boys had swiftly emerged from their parents' basements to hurl all sorts of online vulgarity at me from behind the safe anonymity of fake Twitter handles with photos of Ger-man storm troopers and fatalistic Nietzsche quotes. They marched in lockstep as if on cue, to call me *vile* and *evil* and to let me know that my "Jewishness" was showing. (Never mind that I'm not Jewish; however, Jesus *was,* but that's another conversation for another day.) They began to inundate me with all sorts of hypothetical situations in which my son and some imaginary Muslim boy were both hanging from a ledge and I could only save one of them—an imagined moral "gotcha" illustrating what they believed to be the inherent flaws of my position.

These responses weren't a surprise coming from such social media Fourth Reichers, who view everything and everyone through the lens of their perceived (and unearned) superiority based on their GPS location at the time of birth. This kind of entitled bigotry is their daily bread and butter, the heart of the gospel of American superiority that they've embraced. I expect hatred of people of color and of foreigners from them, the way I count on AC/DC for perfect three-minute, four-chord, fist-pumping, stadium-shaking anthems. It's what they do.

The more revelatory and surprising negative feedback came from people like Amy, a professed "God and Country" mom who replied to the same tweet, "John, if you have children, I feel sorry for them that you don't care for them more than some kid in Syria." Her words echoed a similar outpouring from self-identified Bible-believing, God-fearing Jesus folk, punctuated by lots of venom, familiar Fox News cut-and-paste criticisms of Islam, and of course lots of references to *making America great,* as Jesus would. These Christians (who supposedly worship a Middle Eastern rabbi who was born in a feeding trough and spirited away soon after birth by parents fleeing genocide) rushed to join the pseudo-fascists in affirming the idea that children in Syria are not as important as their child, that humanity is not of universal value, and that America is indeed God's priority—seemingly oblivious to the red flag that such agreement should raise if they were paying attention. They shouldn't be on the same side of anything with Nazis, and yet here they were, defending the same scary territory.

Their commonalities were a symptom of the heart sickness many American Christians have inherited

BELIEVING THAT GOD SHOWS NO FAVORITISM

LOVING PEOPLE AS JESUS DID

or learned, one revealed in a growing Christian nationalism as well as a strange, highly selective pro-life position in
which life isn't just more valuable inside the womb than outside of it, but also more valuable inside America than outside
of it. At the core of this inconsistency is a deeply embedded, subconscious belief that a child *is* of greater worth if
their trip through the birth canal happens to deposit them
within our borders rather than outside of them. For them,
even if they can't verbalize it or are not aware of it, "American" is synonymous with "sacred." Amy's response and the
responses of many white Christians to my tweet were telling.
They assume that love for one must come at the expense
of another; they reflect a fearful religion that suggests they
are perpetually in danger; and they reveal a faith rooted in
superiority and self-preservation, one that breeds hostility
to those it sees as outsiders—which turns out to be an awful
lot of people.

Far too much of American evangelicalism has become
this—and it's a problem. It's a problem because the lin-
eage of our Christian tradition leads back to Moses being
saved from Pharaoh's ethnic cleansing of the Jewish people.
It's a problem because the story of the Israelites is one of
continual escape from violent oppression as marginalized,
despised foreigners. It's a problem because Jesus was born
to temporary refugees desperately fleeing genocide. It's a
problem because the core of his teaching was the greatest
commandment (not the greatest suggestion) to love your
neighbor as yourself—and that designation of *neighbor* had
nothing to do with geography or nationality but with shared
divinity-reflecting humanity. To claim the Christian faith is
to aspire to practice the most radical kind of hospitality and
the most counterintuitive compassion for the other. Jesus
was an itinerant street preacher who modeled sacrificial

love and who welcomed to his table both beggar and soldier, both priest and prostitute, both Jew and Samaritan.
It's impossible to simultaneously emulate *this* Jesus while
championing exclusion, localized supremacy, pigmented
superiority, or bordered empathy. If we want love to be our
calling card again, we're going to have to tattoo this on our
hearts, preach it from our pulpits, and tweet it every day
until it takes hold in us. We're going to have to acknowledge
that God is international, multicultural, and globalist.

And that's the heart of this for Americans who profess a Christian faith: eventually you have to choose. You
simply cannot be both "for God so loved the world"—and
"America First." One of these declarations will have to
yield. You can't preach an *all-people* gospel while despising
refugees and foreigners and immigrants, as these are contra-
dictory movements. You can't claim that "all lives matter"
while protecting only those who share your pigmentation.
You cannot be fully pro-life and uphold your supremacy
based on color, geography, or religion. You either believe
that all people are made fully in the image of God without
exception—or you don't. You either aspire to a benevolence
without conditions or caveats or border or color codes—
or you can't bring yourself to. It's morally impossible to
simultaneously pledge complete allegiance to both Jesus
and America. At some point one will win out, and when
your religious position on foreigners begins to align with a
malevolent fascist extremist—it may be time to reconsider
your interpretation of the gospel. It may be time to see if
you've made God in your own American, Caucasian image.

I don't imagine that Amy, the "God and Country"
mom, or the Christians like her would say they have anything
in common with a blatantly racist neo-Nazi like Richard
Spencer, but there is a disturbing congruence in their shared

hostility toward nonwhite, non-Christian non-Americans and in anti-Semitic prejudice. The aggressive territorialism they co-own is alarming, as is their explicit or implied assertion that life is somehow worth more the closer to you it is. There is nothing of Jesus in this. Yes, if God is as big as we claim and as loving as we contend, all life is equally valuable wherever it arrives from or currently resides—and yes, spiritually speaking, a child five thousand miles away *is* as inherently beautiful and worthy of protection as my own—and your own. If you're a Christian and you care to argue with that, go ahead, but you're going to have to argue with Jesus while also aligning yourself with white supremacy as you do. (I'm not sure that's a good spot to plant your theological flag, and I know it's a lousy way to spread the message of Jesus' love beyond the relatively small 16.3 percent of the world's real estate America occupies.) There is no border on real compassion and there aren't varying degrees of human worth either—no matter what Richard Spencer or Amy or Steve Bannon or Donald Trump say or believe. If America *is* first, Jesus can only be a very distant second. For those of us trying to love people as Jesus loved them—that just won't do.

Chapter 7
OH, HELL NO!

"I miss hell."

It was a startling admission coming from the longtime pastor of a thousand-member church in a bustling neighborhood just inside the West Philadelphia city limits, a few short minutes before a Sunday morning service. He'd punctuated the statement with a deep, throaty laugh, but he wasn't joking as much he was marveling at the admission coming out of his mouth. "Hell was helpful," he said, his face growing solemn. "When I could leverage sin and hold eternal damnation over people's heads, I could get them to do almost anything: volunteer, give, evangelize, vote—whatever needed doing." He explained that this fear was a kind of currency, a sanctified, ordained, and acceptable tool of explicit or just-below-the-radar spiritual extortion. He went on to tell me that when his own faith shifted and his community slowly transitioned with him to a more progressive theology, he lost the ability to energize people easily through existential threat—and in a way he missed having something similarly catalytic to collectively move his people, lamenting that his congregation (while filled with engaged human beings who care deeply about the world) was far more passive than it had been before they got out of the condemnation business.

This is why the conservative evangelical movement in America is able to marshal its rank and file to vote for extremist candidates, to embrace nonsensical conspiracy theories, to tolerate abhorrent behavior from leaders, or to justify seemingly conflicting cruelty toward people: they're terrified of getting it wrong and pissing off God. The fear of eternal torment (or the impulse to help other less-righteous souls avoid it) tends to drive religious people beyond what seems reasonable to more moderate believers or to the irreligious—and while it may be effective in mobilizing evangelistic outreach or moving voting blocs, it does little to perpetuate anything truly loving because it values conversion over conversation. Beyond that, it's also driving an exodus out of organized religion, and we can't ignore that.

LIVING SCARED OF HELL

MISSING OUT ON A LIFE OF LOVE

But as people of faith, morality, and conscience, more than simply recognizing this unhealthy preoccupation with punching the ticket out of hell, we also need to provide an equally compelling alternative—something built around a different kind of urgency. We need to create communities where deeply spiritual human beings can gather, people who know that for hungry people salvation is a plate of rice and beans, and for exhausted sea-battered migrants it is a soft bed on solid ground. The future of organized religion has got to be built on something more redemptive than damnation avoidance. It has to be able to activate people over something besides escaping wrath, because those returns are ever diminishing and really easy to weaponize against those we don't like.

I was talking with a group of teenagers at our church, and one of them was sharing the tensions he was feeling with a friend whose caustic phobias about LGBTQ people frustrated him. He said, "I honestly feel like everything he believes and does is because he's afraid of going to hell and thinks this will protect him. It's like he's scared of God." That teen is on to something.

Doesn't the existence of hell seem incompatible with the character of a God whose defining trait is love, anyway? What is ultimately loving about inflicting suffering on someone you supposedly have limitless affection for, no matter what the reason? Jesus does paint a vivid and frightening picture of a painful place disconnected from God[1] (though this idea is largely absent elsewhere in Scripture); however, translating such imagery into the trenches of daily life is a daunting and fruitless task. I think the road to hell is paved with the idea of hell. Once we sign on to it as a reality, the next decision we need to make is: Who goes there and why do they go there? What are the precise rules and fine print of damnation? Is a profession of faith or sinner's prayer required for a reprieve, or does it depend on how you treat vulnerable people? Is deliverance based on belief or behavior? The Bible makes the case for both (Mark 16:16; Matthew 25:31–46), with the Gospel writers offering very different replies—so how do we decide where salvation is and who gets to enjoy it? If we can't reach a clear consensus regarding how a reservation to hell is secured, maybe we should hold that idea loosely and be reluctant to wield it as a weapon. Every second we spend trying to decode Jesus' poetic word pictures about what happens after we die is another second we could be obediently embodying his prolific and very explicit directions on equity, forgiveness, generosity, and social justice: the making of heaven here on earth. Like Jesus, anything carrying the name *Christian* needs to leave people with more dignity and greater care, with healed wounds and fuller bellies, with calmed fears and quieted worries. It needs to leave people seen and heard and known. Like the life of Jesus, it needs to leave a wake of kindness and goodness and compassion. If we are perpetually burdened to share and to heal and to restore while we're here and trust that God's love is something nothing can separate us from, we can trust in the after-party too.

So there I was on a sunny Sunday afternoon at the local dog park, gingerly tiptoeing through a cluttered minefield of steaming canine care packages alongside our eight-year-old Dutch Shepherd mix, Zoe, discussing the eternal destinations of human souls with complete strangers, as one does—and I was about to step in it royally. A few moments earlier I'd met a young couple chaperoning their affable, slightly skittish terrier pup, and we allowed our furry children to introduce themselves with an exchange of hindquarter sniffs and adorable play bows. After a brief smattering of small talk with the couple I told them what I did for a living, and as happens frequently we began chatting about our shared Christian faith. They told me they were students at the local Southern Baptist seminary and my spidey sense started going off, and for good reason. Barely three minutes into our conversation, the woman smiled widely and in a strange non sequitur said, "I'm just so grateful to God because he loved me when I deserved hell." I'd heard words like this a few hundred times before, of course, but encountering them here without the supporting context of a church service or Bible study, they were particularly jarring to my ears and triggered a knee-jerk reply that launched immediately from my lips without giving me time to edit or soften it.

"You did?" I asked. "You deserved hell . . . just for being born?"

"Yes," she responded matter-of-factly, as if the question didn't faze her in the slightest. "The Bible says that I was born sinful and separated from God because of it."

I pressed her, knowing this could be a messy proposition, but our dogs were getting along well and I took a chance. "So, God lovingly made you and gave you life and placed you here in the middle of a world you've never been to—but despised you out of the chute for something two people supposedly did millions of years before you were ever born? God held a grudge against you for the failing of your ancient ancestors?"

"No." She tried to clarify as if I'd misunderstood. "God *loved* me so he sent Jesus to save me from my sin."

Clearly this was not going well. I think Zoe sensed it too, because she pulled me sharply toward the exit, but I resisted and pressed on, much to her consternation. "But, couldn't God have just forgiven you (and all of us) preemptively, *without* needing Jesus and his death, and without you needing to believe any of this or pray any prayer?" I continued, without pausing very long for a response. "Couldn't he just have forgiven and forgotten—and if not, isn't he really just saving you from himself then, anyway?"

Things got awkward. There was a protracted silence, the husband looked uncomfortable, and I'm pretty sure I saw Zoe roll her eyes. This was the kind of mess you can't easily scrape from the bottom of your shoe with a stick, and I was hoping one of the dogs might relieve themselves to break the tension. Before I could fill the uncomfortable quiet with more words, the woman managed a strained smile before making an awkward exit, with her puppy (and husband, who I later realized never actually said a word) following behind. I hadn't meant to be flippant or disrespectful to her, but I also realized how my questions had been received because I'd been on the other side of them back when I was living comfortably in orthodoxy and overconfident in an inherited narrative that I hadn't scrutinized. I had just pushed back on a story she loved and had invested herself in and really wanted to be true, and my probing questions weren't just uncomfortable interrogations—they were an existential threat, a spiritual attack she'd been warned about by pastors and church friends and celebrity evangelists. She'd had a run-in with an actual heretical radical leftist who she fears is condemned. She felt sorry for me. I reciprocated.

You need to check a lot of boxes in order to condemn someone to hell: you need to believe in God, to imagine you know that God's character intimately, to consent to that God manufacturing a place where that God would send human beings for a gruesome and torturous eternity, to be fully certain you know the extensive and precise requirements for such a sentence, to be sure the person you're condemning meets those requirements, and, above all, to be fully convinced that you don't. I'll argue that if someone reaches all these standards, they're likely God—and if they don't (and still have the nerve to tell someone they're going to hell) they're likely an insufferable human being. It's almost impossible to love your neighbor as yourself if you believe that your neighbor is in some unrepentant sin that disqualifies them from proximity to a God you have intimacy with. Holding hell over

AN EXPANDED UNDERSTANDING OF GOD'S LOVE

SEEING YOUR INHERENT GOODNESS

someone renders you unable to have the kind of closeness to them that love requires, the kind that sees people accurately.

I've lived a good deal of my formative years quite sure that hell was real and trying desperately to figure out how to avoid it. It was simply something I accepted as part of my Christianity Starter Kit and incorporated into my religious worldview, my default theology, and my working spirituality. It shaped my understanding of myself and it guided the agenda I approached others with, sometimes turning me into an oxymoronic, self-hating jerk. But with each passing day over the past decade or so, little by little, I've started to feel the erosion of the unwavering certainty of something that had once seemed so critical and nonnegotiable to my belief system, yet which had grown more and more paradoxical in my mind: *eternal damnation at the hands of a supposedly loving God.* At this state of my spiritual journey and in my current understanding of the character of God and my study of the Scriptures, I simply no longer can reconcile these two things. As hard as I have tried to (and believe me, as a good and guilty Catholic boy at heart, I have), I just do not have peace with a Creator who would give us life and force us to spend much of that life looking for a spiritual needle in a haystack to avoid torture for eternity in the name of fierce love. This unbelief is not a conscious decision and it hasn't come without decades of prayer, study, and reflection, so I can't be argued or prooftexted out of it and I won't be shamed out of it either. It's more of a yielding to the involuntary response of my heart as I have walked in faith and lived life seeking Jesus.

I'd certainly wrestled with these issues before my doggie park come-to-Jesus meeting, but encountering this young woman and hearing her confession of faith there in the fading light of a fall afternoon surrounded by dogs and their human handlers framed it all in a way that finally called out in all-caps bold type what I'd had so much unrest about: she believes she's inherently dirty and deserving of punishment. *Amazing grace, how sweet the sound, that saved a wretch like me!* Humanity's depravity is one of the central pillars of the faith story for her and so many people. There's something so very sad about that to me now, not only because it places a voice in our head that condemns us, but because it makes us far more likely to condemn and judge other people who really just need our loving presence in the middle of lives that already come with a good deal of collateral damage. This woman walking her dog and speaking with me that afternoon had lived this *very* God story quite passionately—one centered around her own inherent sickness. I had lived it too. Millions upon millions of Christians have and are living it right now. I just can no longer be one of them and be honest at the same time.

I realize many of you are saying, "But John, that's the heart of the Christian story: creation, the fall, people missing the mark, and God sending Jesus to remove the penalty of sin." I know that to say otherwise is heresy to some of you. I get it. It's been my story since I can remember, but I'm less convinced than ever that it's helpful in producing better human beings or making the planet more loving.

And yes, if this *is* your current story please know that I respect your journey, but before you Google my email or search me on social media so that you can launch the sacred grenades of favorite Scripture quotes at me, know that I have already read them all, studied them, unpacked them, taught them, lived with them for twenty years—and literally designed, printed, and bought the T-shirt. That the concept of hell is part of a great many Christians' orthodoxy and a staple of recent Church history isn't revelatory—and it isn't going to alter my conclusions either. I once heard it said that there is a truth that you cannot argue us out of once we have experienced it. This is the spot from which I speak and believe now, even though there is unsteadiness. In the quiet places where I seek and pray and encounter God, the *deep that calls to deep*[2] says: "There is no fear in Me. You are beloved. I delight in you." You can mount violent assaults of systematic theology and dogmatic doctrine, and they will not be louder than this voice. All the finger wagging and threat throwing and pulpit pounding will likely fail to scare the hell into me. You can label me a false prophet and prodigal rebel, and I will rest in the reality that I am simply an honest and stumbling disciple trying to find the truest truth and live it. And if my heart is mistaken in all of this, I trust that the One who I so strain to hear will know more than any human being the depths to which I have been seeking and the earnestness of my desires, and will give me safe passage to whatever glory looks like. If perfect, fear-expelling love *is* real, this is what it looks like; a forgiveness more relentless than my failings.

Yes, friend, you and I are most certainly flawed and fractured and all sorts of jacked up in ways that sometimes make other people rightly run from us—but I do not believe we are fundamentally despicable. We are not born wretched. We are not enemies of God upon conception. We are not filthy from the womb based on the actions of two people who preceded us by millions of years. And we do *not* deserve eternal punishment and neither does anyone else simply *because*. I think if we loosen our grip on that damnation story, we'll find ourselves far less likely to treat other people like hell. That feels like a touch of heaven.

Chapter 8
LET THEM EAT CAKE

I'm not sure what it is about cake that terrifies so many phobic God-followers. Maybe it's the gluten; a lot of people seem to have issues with it. The past few years have seen a precipitous rise in news stories and legal cases like that of the Masterpiece Cakeshop,[1] involving professed Christians refusing to make wedding cakes for LGBTQ couples, on the grounds that such an act is incompatible with their religious convictions. I also recently came across the story of a fifteen-year-old girl who was expelled from her Kentucky Christian school because of a social media post shared by her mother: a picture of the girl sitting in front of the rainbow birthday cake she'd requested to celebrate the occasion with her family.[2] School officials determined that the photo of the teenager (who was also wearing a rainbow-striped shirt) suggested her affinity with a subversive agenda and sent a problematic message not in line with the school's theological stance. I was struck by the absurdity of the fact that *the rainbow was a red flag to Christians.* There's a tragic irony when the Old Testament story's visible symbol of God's expansive, overwhelming love for all humanity (albeit after a pretty horrifying display of anger) becomes an image to rally against and use to exclude. It underscores the irrational fear at the heart of loveless religion: a fifteen-year-old with a cake could be deemed a threat necessitating expulsion—and worse, they could decide this is somehow a loving and God-honoring response.

How does a person or an organization or a denomination professing belief in Divinity defined by grace become so terrified of another human being based on their gender identity, the color of their skin, their sexual orientation, their nation of origin, that they will push them to the periphery of community and ultimately expel them? It's usually handed-down hatred that's come to seem normal. People are weaned on a generational bigotry to which they gradually become acclimated to. This kind of exclusion is the rotten fruit of an inherited narrative of the dangerous outsider perpetuated in so much Bible Belt Christianity: the *foreign* (in any number of definitions) threat quickly advancing and sure to overcome the good, god-fearing, homegrown "normal" folks. So much of evangelical preaching, partisan Right media, and conservative politics subsists on this story of imminent threat. Inherent in this mythos is the assumption of Caucasian, American, Republican, and heteronormative as the moral baseline: a redacted and whitewashed "chosen people" who are fulfilling God's noble agenda to make the USA great. It is a variation on a theme that fundamentalists of many religions wield in supposed defense of God and God's people—for whom they always consider themselves standard-bearers and whose ways they are sole defenders of—justifying whatever measures they deem necessary, no matter how cruel or discriminatory they may seem or actually are. On this perceived moral high ground, doing something like subjecting a teenage girl to the humiliation and sudden, disorienting upheaval of being uprooted from her peers becomes not only reasonable, but righteous.

It's disconcerting enough when someone commits an injurious act and says that the devil made them do it—but it's something far more stomach-turning when they claim that God did. Such malicious discrimination in the name of faith, like that experienced by this Kentucky teenager, loudly reminds the watching world already skeptical of religious people and institutions that there are few human beings as unthinkably malevolent and reactionary as those professing to emulate a compassionate, openhearted Jesus. This kind of paradoxical theology allows people to diverge almost completely from the very heart of the movement they're supposedly seeking to embody, while simultaneously

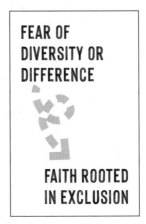

FEAR OF DIVERSITY OR DIFFERENCE

FAITH ROOTED IN EXCLUSION

riding on a high horse of self-righteousness. In the incubator of this straight, white, America-centered theology, of course nationalism rises up, of course homophobia and transphobia are going to take hold, and of course pious people are going to be terrified enough to be triggered by a Technicolor birthday cake and feel the need to separate a young woman from her peer community. Amazingly, the devil is no longer a talking, fruit-peddling serpent or a supernatural manipulator tempting Jesus on a high mountain, but a tenth grader with a love for bold-colored confections. When your God shrinks, your demons tend to multiply, which is a good way to spot people with an undersized deity: what or who do they want to eliminate?

Subjecting someone to that kind of exclusion and expulsion for who they love or their gender identity (or even for their ally-ship with vulnerable communities) isn't just nonsensical at a base level—practically speaking, it's really lousy evangelism, terrible PR, and bad sin-fixin'. You'd think that if you did in fact believe that being gay was a sin, or that same-gender couples were perverting God's plan for marriage, or that transgender teens were in danger of eternal damnation—your greatest and most pressing burden would be to keep LGBTQ human beings tethered to genuine, loving, abiding community. If they were indeed on a narrow road to certain death, I imagine you'd probably want them connected to a church where they could experience the limitless love of your God in close proximity—instead of sharp rejection, swift removal, and finger-pointing from a distance. People outside of organized religion see how ridiculously counterintuitive this perpetually frightened expression of faith really is. Whether they believe in God themselves or not, they know that any entity worthy of the title of *Supreme Being* wouldn't draw battle lines over birthday cakes and Starbucks cups and cuss words in movies—only perpetually insecure disciples of a minuscule God whom they really don't trust to do God stuff. Nonreligious people accurately see that pushing someone away is a fairly terrible method of pointing them toward something supposedly life-giving; that wounding them while inviting them into a painful place and then condemning them because they rightly reject it seems like a perverse form of abuse.

I wonder if the officials at the Kentucky school really thought through their response thoroughly or if it was simply an emotional knee-jerk reaction made in the hysteria of the moment or under the pressure of a few influential parents. I wonder if they ever imagined standing inside the skin of the girl they sent away. There are few times more turbulent and disorienting than adolescence, when the need for authentic community is at a fever pitch, and for apparent spiritual leaders to disconnect a young person from that critical source of meaning, in the name of a God who is supposedly made of love, shows a stunning ability to miss the point. That seems to be the modus operandi of fearful religion rising up in these days in America, though: removal. Expel the suspected LGBTQ teen, send back the refugee, wall off the stranger, deny the health coverage, turn away the beggar, silence the dissenter—and yet in the Gospels we see over and over a Jesus who invites in, a working theology of pulling toward, an apologetic of bigger tables and wider embraces. I think people of faith, morality, and conscience need to be the table setters, the bread bakers, and the cake makers—otherwise whatever they believe in will remain too small to really expand their hearts in a way that welcomes and feeds and loves people into loving community, not out of it.

Over the past two decades as a pastor to students, I've sat with and listened to hundreds of LGBTQ young people, and I've had a front-row seat to the violence the Church has manufactured: the depression, self-harm, and isolation it breeds. It's the thing that grieves me perhaps more than anything else I encounter in this work. It's all such a waste that vast resources are expended by Christians continually fighting a battle that bears no redemptive fruit, that actually exacerbates people's marginalization, that generates unnecessary pain—a war that Jesus isn't asking them to wage in the first place. In the totality of the Gospels, Jesus never once condemns or reprimands anyone for their gender identity or sexual orientation. Jesus *did*, however, say hundreds of times that he came to bring help to the poor and oppressed, that those who loved him would care for the least, that they would be fierce lovers of humanity, that they would escort justice and usher in equity. Yet I don't see equal passion about these things from the most phobic of his followers, and that's one of the most profligate sins the Church is guilty of. If evangelicals were just a fraction as burdened to stop poverty, hunger, systemic racism, or bigotry as they are about policing LGBTQ folk's bedrooms, bathrooms, and body parts, we'd have very little poverty or hunger or racism or bigotry—and Jesus' prayer that the earth look more like heaven would be materializing in our midst and a tangible movement of God would be unmistakable. But I guess those *other* things encroach too much on people's places of comfort, that they are more personally inconvenient and far more taxing than simply dismissing a total stranger based on who and how they love and imagining they're being righteous in the process.

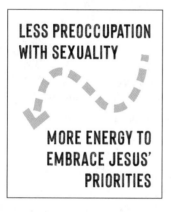

LESS PREOCCUPATION WITH SEXUALITY

MORE ENERGY TO EMBRACE JESUS' PRIORITIES

Every day I grieve the way Christianity is putting LGBTQ people through undue suffering, the callousness of the hearts of so many of those who claim Jesus, and the excuses we make for doing everything but what Jesus actually called us to do. And it sure isn't love.

Few rules exist in the world without exception, but if there's one I've found to universally hold true, it's that if someone is uttering the phrase *Love the sinner, hate the sin*—they're doing it while being abjectly horrible to another human being and trying to make themselves appear far less horrible in the process. Those six words are responsible for more loveless Christianity than any other combination in recorded history— and not surprisingly, they exist nowhere in the teachings

of Jesus or in the early writings of the Church birthed in
the immediate wake of his life. The phrase is a clever inven-
tion of the Religious Right, singularly adopted over the past
few decades by self-identified Christians as an excuse to
exclude LGBTQ human beings from spiritual community,
to justify denial of their civil rights, to defend unthinkable
acts of violence against them—and to allege doing so is an
act of love in the name of a good God.

In some ways, it's a master stroke of sanctified mass
delusion: convince religious people that they are doing
something for a morally compromised person's "own
good," thereby preemptively disqualifying criticism of the
cruelty of their methods or the reasonable objections of
those on the receiving end of their actions. This kind of
theological passing of the buck releases them to participate in otherwise reprehensible behavior because they've
been told in advance that the act is righteous—which is
why professed followers of Jesus can steadfastly insist they
are *loving* LGBTQ people, who are in actuality not feeling at all loved by their words or their ways, but instead
are experiencing trauma in their presence. "Of course they
don't like what I have to say," these self-deputized moral
police officers respond, "sinners never like to face God's
righteous correction." Christians armed with *hate the sin*
as their declared impetus often rationalize their discrimination by comparing themselves to a parent giving a child
"tough love," missing the Olympic-level arrogance of sug-
gesting that adult human beings, whom they often have no
relationship with or knowledge of, require their oversight
or discipline. Even though Jesus instructs his disciples to
use a mirror before a window when looking for immorality to address,[3] these "sinner lovers" can justify fixating

exclusively on someone else and never question whether or not they resemble Jesus in any measure.

When my son Noah was a toddler, rather than telling him I loved him, I began asking him a question: "Who loves you?"—to which he would reply with a beaming smile and great exuberance: "Daddy!" And I'd applaud and smile widely and say, "Yeah he does!" Yes, the question was playfully rhetorical, but rather than just expressing my love for him and assuming it wasn't lost in translation, I wanted to make sure he *felt* loved by me, to know he was receiving what I intended to give him.

I don't think Christians do that often enough with many vulnerable communities, but particularly with the LGBTQ community. We don't simply listen. We tell people they're wrong to feel dehumanized and disregarded, instead of wondering if us making them feel that way is actually the morality issue. The clear and infuriating cognitive dissonance of the Christian perpetrators of phobic violence who insist they're loving LGBTQ human beings despite passionate responses to the contrary from those who identify that way is helpful in thinking about what constitutes a loving act, regardless of our theological leanings or the people on the other end of our exchanges and relationships. Whatever our religious tradition, we usually imagine that we are erring on the side of goodness and decency when encountering people with whom we disagree, simply because we like to think of ourselves as basically good and decent people—but that is only half of the equation. Since we're all understandably prone to self-favoritism, the story we tell ourselves is incomplete without the input of others. Love is fundamentally relational, and we can't evaluate our actions simply by our declarations (I am loving) or our intentions (I want to be loving). We also need to consider the experience of those on the receiving end of our actions (do people *feel* loved by me, and if they don't, specifically why *don't* they?).

The Golden Rule of doing unto others as you would have done to you really begins to break down if someone says that what we're *doing unto them* is hurtful and we ignore it—unless we somehow prefer to be damaged ourselves. If I imagine that I'm a loving husband without ever asking my wife if she actually feels loved by me (or ignoring her if she tells me she doesn't), I'm missing a really important half of the relational equation. I need to be accountable to her as an integral part of our mutually respectful interconnection. The purity or nobility of our intentions alone isn't sufficient no matter how confident we are of them. It doesn't matter how much phobic Christians sincerely believe they're "loving sinners," if they ignore the pain expressed to them by LGBTQ human beings—and it doesn't matter if they tell themselves that they're just confronting immoral behavior in the name of God, if the methods they use inflict greater injury. Jesus never interacts with people as abstract moral principles, but as sacred and unique human beings, and he always affirms their fully specific humanity as his life intersects with theirs. I wonder what "hate the sin" justifications we've made as we've dispensed damnation or wielded judgment or confronted behavior.

Today I received an email similar to one I have received hundreds of times a year. It was from a man I've never met or spoken to before. The names and particulars of these messages vary, but the through line is constant: ostracism, self-hatred, and fear of a supposedly loving God—all provided by hateful Christians.

He wrote:

> I am conflicted. I am a gay, black male and only seek
> God's love, grace, and mercy. I am surrounded by a
> group of people who preach the traditional Baptist
> teaching of hellfire and brimstone. I am daily trying
> to seek God's love and grace, yet I feel that, because
> I am gay, I am not worthy and will never prosper.
> Am I not deserving of happiness? Am I so wrong for
> being gay? I believe that God makes us who we are,
> but Christian people tell me that I am choosing this
> path. What choice? If all is set before my conception,
> then what choice do I have? What am I to do, if God
> knows my moves before I make them? God knows
> the outcome. Where is the truth in this? Religion has
> me broken and I am on an uncertain road. Can you
> provide any words of advice? Does God truly love
> me? Am I to fall under the word of people claiming
> they are prophets, ministers, seers of God—or am I
> just damned completely?

I'm not going to tell you how to respond theologically to
this man and his questions, because in many ways, your
theology is irrelevant—aside from a working apologetic of
empathy that recognizes another person's pain and is burdened to bring comfort. Regardless of what you believe
about sexuality, I'm asking you to consider the suffering of
this man and multitudes like him, the condemnation they
carry, the prevalent fear of God they live with, and then
decide how love would have you respond—to him, and
to millions of similarly wounded people who pass you on
the street, serve you at restaurants, stand behind you in
the checkout line, and fill your social media timeline. The

Gospel of Matthew tells us that Jesus saw the crowds and had compassion on them, "because they were harassed and helpless."[4] He saw their internal condition, what the world was doing to them, how they were affected by this life, and he was moved to bring comfort and rest and wholeness. If you're using the Bible to proof-text yourself into feeling justified for discriminating against someone else, you're probably doing religion and the Bible incorrectly—and you're definitely doing love wrong.

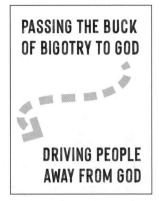

PASSING THE BUCK OF BIGOTRY TO GOD

DRIVING PEOPLE AWAY FROM GOD

The saddest irony of all is that *this* is what the Bible warns against. Jesus' life and ministry pissed off the hypocritical religious phonies who feigned outrage and leveraged faith to prey upon vulnerable people while he dined with prostitutes, tax collectors, and detested street people. The supposedly sanctified resented him precisely because he widened the embrace of God. It was his expanding hospitality and his refusal to deny people affection, proximity, dignity, or respect that made him so hated by those who believed God belonged to them alone. Nothing new under the sun here. Jesus washed the feet of his betrayer. He healed on the Sabbath. He touched the hand of a leper. He dined with the disregarded. He spoke in public with women about spirituality. He made a despised Samaritan the hero in his story. He embraced the outcasts. He gladly fed a disparate, sprawling multitude stretched out before him. Jesus would have made the stupid cake.

He'd be making rainbow cakes and providing refugees sanctuary and welcoming immigrants and giving people health care and doing the things that loving people do regardless of their profession of faith. If Jesus were at the Masterpiece Cakeshop when a same-sex couple walked in, I believe he'd be kind at the sales counter, effusive in his generosity, and overflowing with joy while making the most delicious dessert he could muster, because he knew that ultimately love and compassion—not hatred and exclusion—are what faith should liberate us to, and that if we really trust a big God to do whatever needs doing in people's hearts, we will stop being a barrier to their proximity to that God. Based on the evidence in the Gospels, Jesus would gladly let LGBTQ couples eat cake, no matter how vehemently some Christians carry on otherwise. He'd do that not because nor in spite of who they were. He'd do it because they needed a cake and because making that cake (like every other act Jesus performed) would let them know of their beauty and belovedness. Those of us seeking to perpetuate the audacious heart of Jesus—believing that he meant what he said and how he lived—will keep feeding people with cakes and compassion in generous portions.

Chapter 9
DOPPELGANGER GOD

A few years ago, our family took a trip to Universal Studios Florida. On our inaugural day, one of the first things we did was take in *Shrek 4-D*, which at the time was a novel, if now common, theme park experience: a 3-D movie viewed while being sprayed periodically with air or water and having your seat shaken or tilted to ratchet up the realism. It was billed as an "immersive experience," and my expectations were commensurately stratospheric, given that I had come just short of listing an organ on eBay to cover the cost of the trip. As we finished snaking through the seemingly endless queue and prepared to enter the theater, we each were handed a pair of plastic yellow glasses and ushered quickly into the nearest row of seats. I took off my sunglasses and helped my children get settled in. As the houselights went down and the soundtrack swelled, a jovial voice instructed us to put on our 3-D glasses, and I promptly complied as the movie began. I was ready to be fully immersed into the promised state-of-the-art experience, and after a few seconds—I was not impressed. The picture didn't have the clarity I expected, given the location and price, and my giddy expectancy dissolved into disappointment and a bit of buyer's remorse. I looked around the theater to see if there had been some sort of technical issue, or if anyone else looked as disappointed as I was—but they all seemed perfectly fine. I pitied them all for their low entertainment standards and prayed God would supernaturally upgrade their expectations. I then turned to my wife, who I can often count on to mirror my displeasure in such circumstances, but she was beaming. "Well, she married me," I thought to myself, "so really, who can account for her taste?" For the next six or seven minutes I impatiently endured what I had decided was a subpar, overpriced waste of precious park time, until the film finally ended to unanimous (sans one) uproarious applause and the houselights came back up. As I stood up and prepared to vacate my seat for the next waiting vacationers, my wife looked at me oddly, pointed at the top of my head, and asked, "What's that?" I put my hands to where she'd directed me and felt the unmistakable thin pieces of plastic I was handed seven minutes earlier upon entry, and my mind whirled as I realized what had happened: as we'd entered the dark theater, in my excitement I'd inadvertently placed the 3-D glasses on top of my head—and watched the entire film in a dark room with my ordinary sunglasses. My wife (who, as you can imagine, for many reasons is long-suffering) caught her breath after nearly hyperventilating with laughter and said with a roll of her eyes, "Let's go back around and get in line again." I responded like a first grader being told we could keep the puppy we'd found on the side of the road. We exited the building and returned immediately to the queue we'd occupied thirty minutes before. This time as we entered, I took careful note of the whereabouts of my respective glasses and as the houselights once again dimmed, I secured the right pair over my eyes. It was a magical, immersive experience.

The lenses through which we view the world matter. As we live in community alongside disparate people, it's tempting to imagine that everyone sees things as we do, that their filters match our own, that we are having a similar experience of the same planet, the same country, the same religion, even the same Jesus. But the truth is, we each have incredibly specific story-shaped lenses that subjectively inform and color and alter life in front of us. You carry yours with you into the places you live and work and navigate on your phone (even as you encounter these words)—which is why spirituality and politics are both so messy and fraught with discord: because 2.7 billion separate sacred, beloved stories are colliding every day. That's a ton of relational friction to sustain, whether we're deeply religious, decidedly undecided, or passionately antireligion. And for those of us who *do* consider ourselves believers in some capacity, we face a fundamental problem in thinking and talking about religion: we all make "God" either slightly or substantially in our own image.

This subjective and self-referential picture of the Divine is formed by the homes and families in which we were raised, the teachers we had, the faith communities we did or didn't grow up in, our individual life experiences, our personality types, and even our very physicality. These differences alter the way in which we view the world as it relates to spiritual things and to the working theology we practice. Those of us who have engaged Christianity either directly or peripherally all sift the words and the life of Jesus for those parts of them that seem to reflect our passions, confirm our prejudices, ratify our politics, and echo the story we tell ourselves. Because those lenses have shaped the Gospel stories we've read and have had preached to us, we tend to worship a God of Confirmation Bias. Every person claiming to be a Christian or simply aspiring to the teachings of Jesus has a highly personalized, greatly customized, individually constructed, and ultimately incomplete Jesus.

There are as many Jesuses in this world as there are people claiming belief in him, as many as there are Christians reading this book.

Even when we use the Bible as our apparent place of commonality, we bring our extremely precise selves to that singular story and create an entirely unique take on the narrative that tends to correspond with our own. That's why one person can read the New Testament story of Jesus about to be unjustly arrested in the garden, instructing his disciples to come back and "bring a sword," and say, "*This* is why I can have my guns and defend myself," and believe it aligns them with Jesus and is faith affirming, while another person can read a few paragraphs ahead in the very same story—where Peter cuts off a slave's ear, Jesus rebukes him, heals the man, and tells them his people will not live by the sword—and say, "*This* is why a follower of Jesus has no business possessing a deadly weapon or using physical violence."[1] Same story, same Jesus—completely disparate views on guns, violence, protection, and self-defense. Or, as another example, one person can read in the Gospel of Mark that Jesus spoke of marriage and said, "For this reason a man shall leave his father and mother and be joined to his wife,"[2] and believe Jesus was confirming the union as strictly between a man and a woman—while another person can note that not once in the Gospels does Jesus criticize or condemn anyone based on their gender identity or sexual orientation and believe that Jesus would be fully LGBTQ affirming. Same Gospels. Same Jesus.

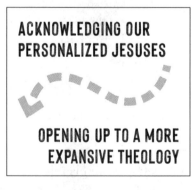

ACKNOWLEDGING OUR PERSONALIZED JESUSES

OPENING UP TO A MORE EXPANSIVE THEOLOGY

Completely different faith-informed, biblically justified perspective on sexuality, marriage, gender.

This is true of every possible area of our lives, not just the obvious culture-war issues. We Christians can't help but read the Gospels so they skew our way, which is why, in the stories we encounter there, we almost always imagine that we're Jesus—or at the very least, that we're the earnest, faithful disciples alongside him and never the self-righteous religious frauds whose hypocrisy he's condemning. We like to picture ourselves as the Good Samaritan rescuing the wounded man on the roadside—not those callous people walking by. We're always the persecuted woman, never the chastised stone-throwers.[3] We're always like Jesus and never a jerk. This bias toward ourselves is a huge obstacle, and it impacts us greatly that we have such disparate images of God or Jesus, because if we are serious about living our faith, this image of God or portrait of Jesus forms the primary lens through which we view everything: our relationships, the environment, the church, equality, health care, politics, parenting—the way we experience this life.

If having a personalized Jesus is a challenge to each of us individually as we relate to one another, it's even more difficult if we're going to try to live in spiritual community locally and as part of the bigger Church in the world. If a community bears the name "Christian"—whether it's five of us or fifty of us or five hundred or five thousand—we have to somehow figure out which version of Jesus we are going to emulate in the world together, which understanding of God we are going to perpetuate together. That's the mess we're in not just in this room but in denominations across America. In many local churches, the Black Lives Matter

movement in response to police brutality, the separation of
families at our southern border, and the deaths in the wake
of this pandemic have turned the already present hairline
fractures into compound breaks that simply can no longer
be denied. We've had to reckon with other people's lenses
and other people's Jesuses and to admit the disconnect.

The Gospel writer John shares the story of Jesus calling himself the Good Shepherd.[4] He reminds us that Jesus
is far more complex than we are usually comfortable with.
Yes, he is the tender shepherd to the sheep—to those he
sees as harassed and helpless, he *is* a gentle and compassionate pastoral presence—but not to the wolves, not to the
religious leaders and the power holders and the predators.
To them he is a holy terror. To those personally and collectively threatening the sheep, he is a fierce and public adversary. In both this description of himself and in his public
life and ministry, Jesus is both compassionate personal caregiver and radical system influencer. He is learner of stories
and status quo challenger. He is both pastor and activist,
table setter and table overturner.

Can we make room for these very different Jesuses?
Can we embrace the Jesus who withdrew to quiet places to
pray and the one who made a whip out of cords and confronted the temple vendors? Can we balance the shepherd
Jesus with the activist Jesus, the one who said, "Love your
enemies," and the one who said, "Love the least"? Likewise,
can we imagine ourselves as recipients of both his tender
care and his sharp critique? Can we find the fullest, deepest
understanding of what it means to be Christian and try to
manifest that at this place and time in the history of the planet?
That's the scale of the kind of love we're talking about here.

Most of us have heard the phrase *God is love*, which
is true because both are nearly impossible to quantify with

words or comparisons to anything else. "God is like . . ." That's the problem, isn't it? Whatever answers we come up with, whatever words or attributes or ideas feel at all accurate, are going to be woefully incomplete. We may find language that helps us, but in the same way that numbers can only orient us toward the infinite, words only provide a direction for us to walk toward the Spirit. As a pastor writing and speaking about the ineffable, the best I can hope for is to draw upon every aspect of life—nature and emotion and experience and longing and love—and somehow tap into some elemental, transcendent part of being human, and then use that humanity to point toward the Divinity.

Most of the time we find ourselves anthropomorphizing God. We can't help but attach human characteristics or touchstones to whatever holds this all together—and that's usually where trouble starts, because we use the mirror as a reference point more than anything else. Susan B. Anthony once said, "I distrust those who know so well what God wants because I notice it coincides with their own desires." The Bible doesn't shy away from this danger.

Jonah is a good example of this. He's a rather petty prophet, if you ask me. He gets more credit than perhaps he should, because he's got a cool backstory with some pretty memorable special effects. Despite what our children's books and Sunday school teachers have led us to believe, the narrative of Jonah *isn't* about a grown man using a giant fish as a three-day Airbnb; it's about a bitter religious zealot who wants God to hate the people he hates, and avoids a diety who he suspects has a far bigger heart than he does—and he doesn't want to yield to it. (Actually, come to think of it, I kinda get *that* guy.) To avoid bringing the message of God's expansive love to the Ninevites (whom he despises), he runs away, becomes a ship stowaway, ends up tossed in the ocean at his own request—and gets swallowed up by the aforementioned fish for his lost weekend stuck in darkness, seawater, and krill remains. In fact, Jonah's contempt for the Ninevites is so great that when God inevitably comes through and shows a benevolence wide enough to embrace them in their

CONFRONTING SELF-PORTRAIT RELIGION

RECOGNIZING YOUR OWN MORAL BLIND SPOT

obstinacy and immorality, he sulks like a fourth grader and openly resents the grace they receive. "I knew it!" he scolds his Maker. "I knew you'd let them off the hook and do that whole forgiving thing, and *this* is why I was trying to avoid this entire briny, stinking disaster!" Jonah didn't really want to love his neighbor as much as he wanted his neighbor to feel the wrath of a God who was as angry and vengeful as he was. I *really* get that guy.

We see a similar response in the parable of the Prodigal Son, whose older brother bristles at his father's effusive welcome to his rebellious younger sibling.[5] He doesn't just want to be loved himself; he wants others to be denied it. That's the painful truth about forgiveness: it's rarely God who's reticent to let people into the eternally opened arms of restorative grace—it's usually us.

It's funny how the Almighty's prejudices and biases end up mirroring our own, how similarly petty and vindictive the God in our heads becomes. We might say that we believe in grace as an abstract religious concept, but when the rubber meets the road and we encounter people who boil our blood and draw our disdain and trigger our sensitivities, we (like Jonah) resist accepting them for fear that this will mean they're getting away with something. We withhold community and inclusion from them, not because we really believe God would do this, but because we want to punish them for not meeting our standards, retaliating through distance or disconnection. We ironically push people away to show them how they failed to be as loving as we are. In the Gospel stories, the religious leaders were often similarly outraged when Jesus' compassion eclipsed their own: when the lepers, beggars, nonbelievers, screwups, and sinners received the same embrace and the same regard that the "good and righteous people" did. It was their desire to hoard blessing and withhold mercy that rendered them unable to practice a bigger love than they were comfortable with.

That's one of the greatest challenges in the spiritual journey: to keep seeking to emulate the character of a God who will always outlove you, outforgive you, outwelcome you. The daily task of the believer is to lean into the acts of kindness and hospitality that you most resist, toward the people you least want to bless—to aspire to a place just slightly higher than you feel capable of reaching, because that's how renovation happens, within and around you.

If we claim to be people of faith (as incarnations of Jesus and image-bearers of God) when we resist someone's presence or withhold community or deny them provision, we're declaring explicitly or implicitly that God does not approve of them on some level, and in doing so we're declaring them separate and distinct from the exclusive tribe of the insiders in the process. In that moment, we are simultaneously stating our oneness with God and a separateness from them and that will cause us to withhold love.

For a community, movement, or human being to be in the likeness of whoever or whatever God is, it has to deepen our connections, acknowledge our commonalities, and reinforce our interdependence. Religion at its best will strengthen the tethers between one person and every other human being and to the planet itself, because we recognize that we're all made of the same stuff; we are universally composed of Divinity, equally saturated with Godness. When we do that, separation and tribalism begin to vanish in the presence of something transcendent. There can no longer be a binary dualism of the *in* and the *out*, there can't be *us* and *them*; there is simply a single tribe that we belong to, and we are at home there simply because we breathe. I really want you to see the God *in* you. Just try really hard not to see God *as* you.

Chapter 10
GOOD BOOK,
LOUSY HAMMER

I often hear conservative Christians say that they're "Bible believing" or that they worship a "biblical God," and though they're usually referencing a decidedly male interpretation, I'm never quite sure what else they mean (as it always means something different to each of them). I am, however, fully certain that they don't literally want a God who is completely *biblical,* because by the letter of the law that's probably going to inevitably be uncomfortable for them.

Strictly speaking, a biblical God has a falling out with the first two people He makes, holds a grudge, and levies a permanent penalty against them and everyone else who came after them for ignoring instructions and sampling some explicitly excluded fruit.[1] Rather quickly in the narrative, a biblical God grows so exasperated with the humanity He fashioned in His own image that He determines the only reasonable course of action (among a surely infinite number of available possibilities) is to drown everyone on the planet, with the exception of one extended family and a boatload of animals.[2] An Old Testament biblical God sanctions the thorough and malicious slaughtering of an entire city that was defiant toward Him.[3] A biblical God allows a perennially faithful man like Job to have his life decimated with suffering and grief, just to prove he can handle it.[4] Yes, God emancipates the Israelites, but God also allows them to be enslaved over and over again for generations. If we're honest, going literally by the accounts in the Scriptures, at times a biblical God could easily be described by those unfamiliar with the Bible (who aren't as willing or able to perform mental gymnastics to defend it) as an eternal grudge holder, an easily angered egomaniac, a cruel and detached judge, an insecure and needy stalker. Most people don't want *that* biblical a God; they want the God of the verses they're comfortable with and aware of. They want a very selectively biblical God.

By the same token, many self-professed Christians aren't particularly interested in emulating a biblical Jesus, either: feeding the hungry, elevating the poor, welcoming the foreigner, abolishing retributive violence—that invasive, costly stuff. If Jesus stands in opposition to our American Dream or competes with our 401(k) or rattles our places of comfort or requires sacrifice or asks us to love people we find unlovable—that's a bit more biblical than we're willing to be.

Not long ago I posted a YouTube video, making a case that the Bible never unequivocally declares *homosexuality to be a sin* as so many Christians claim, that there are no words or verses capable of encompassing the vast and complex nature of sexuality and gender identity, and so making a statement that the Bible *does* is a gross oversimplification and cannot be justified scripturally with some simple smoking-gun clobber verse that ends the discussion.[5] A woman named Donna made the comment, the likes of which you've surely heard or perhaps even offered some variation of at one time or another, "Everyone sins." She wrote, "Gay people are no worse than adulterers or thieves or liars. God loves *all* sinners, which is why the penalty for Adam and Eve was death—but we were given Jesus!" In her mind she was being gracious toward LGBTQ people by acknowledging a love bigger than their supposed transgressions (which seems, on its face, to be better than outright homophobic hatred). The problem is that she was tossing all LGBTQ human beings into the same "container" of sinister and soiled people who are actively doing harm to others, creating a false equivalency between someone's identity or orientation (or even their loving relationship) and cheaters and thieves and liars. Not only is this a complete disregard of the hundreds of millions of people who don't fit into the narrow confines of cisgender or heterosexual norms, but with that as her operating premise, it is going to be almost impossible for her to really love any LGBTQ person well, because she sees them as specifically morally flawed in a way that she is not. Active superiority is an almost insurmountable obstacle to the kind of love we're called to.

When I tried to share my perspective on the complexities of sexuality and the Bible with Donna further, she drop-quoted Matthew 16:23: "The disciple Peter was scolded by Jesus for 'having on his mind the things of man and not the things of God.' I'm sorry, but I don't believe religion should be based on our feelings." Lost on Donna was the reality that what she was expressing to me was also a *feeling* interpreted by her as objective wisdom. Her aspirations might be noble, her pursuits diligent, and her efforts sincere—but ultimately, she is interacting with words on a page or a screen and reflecting on those words, using her intellect, experiences, influences, and emotions to determine her convictions. This is all any spiritually oriented human beings have ever done and will ever do. No one is really more qualified than anyone else.

As much as we might like to, there is no way to magically download the totality of God's ways directly into our systems so that our decisions and convictions all perfectly echo the mind of the Divinity. No Bible study, sermon series, or church service will give you that. What religious people like Donna are often saying as they chastise others for their theological perspective is "If your conclusions about the character of God or the content of the Scriptures, or your behavior or belief in response to these things, don't suf-

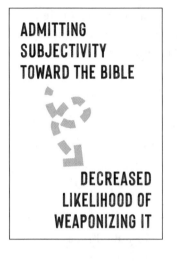

ADMITTING SUBJECTIVITY TOWARD THE BIBLE

DECREASED LIKELIHOOD OF WEAPONIZING IT

ficiently align with mine—I am going to disqualify you for not really having heard or seen as clearly as I have." Loveless religion often comes from deciding someone else's God interpretation is inferior to ours.

Invariably, when a Christian claims to be a "Bible-believing" Christian, they often do so while attempting to dismiss your perspective, diminish your worldview, disqualify your interpretation of Scripture by claiming that *your* authority on the matter at hand is somehow less reliable than their own— because they contend to believe *all* of the Bible and follow *all* of it. *They do not.* They are making the case that the Bible has a simple, irrefutable silver-bullet verse for the topic of the moment, one that silences all discussion and ends any debate. *It rarely does.*

One of the go-to criticisms of these Bible-believing Christians is that the rest of us "cherry-pick" Scripture; they say that we roam through it like a buffet, grabbing huge helpings of what looks good to us and passing by the things we find unpleasant or difficult. *We do. Everyone does. They do too.* That's not to say that we're consciously doing that or that we should intentionally ignore or discard vast portions of the text, but even the most committed and well-intentioned among us, bring something inherently flawed and limited to the table of scholarship and inspiration: ourselves. We all carry our prejudices, fears, experiences, upbringing, and influences along with us to the Bible, and this causes us (even at our very best) to be extremely selective in what we see as gospel, in what we give weight to, in what we practice and amplify and share.

I often find that the people who most weaponize the Bible haven't read all that much of it: just enough to be cruel to people who they resent or are afraid of. For example, in conversations about sexuality, professed Bible-believing Christians will boldly and readily toss out Leviticus 20:13 in conversation, as some supposed sanctified mic drop against the gay community:

> If a man has sexual relations with a man as one does with a woman, both of them have done what is detestable. They are to be put to death; their blood will be on their own heads. (NIV)

Whenever they do, I'll always ask them to kindly move their heads half an inch higher, where the same author in the same chapter of the same book says:

> Anyone who curses their father or mother is to be put to death. Because they have cursed their father or mother, their blood will be on their own head.
> If a man commits adultery with another man's wife—with the wife of his neighbor—both the adulterer and the adulteress are to be put to death.[6]

I ask these people whether they *also* believe that disrespectful teenagers and those committing adultery should be stoned to death. Silence usually follows, or they quickly switch tactics to attack my apparent ignorance regarding the difference between ceremonial law and moral law, or they hop over to the New Testament and drop-quote Paul's letters while ignoring Jesus' silence on the matter.

Or, when discussing the mistreatment of migrant families at our border, a Bible-believing preacher will conveniently ignore the *dozens* of references to welcoming refugees and treating foreigners as one's own, while clinging to a single verse about the wolves coming to kill the sheep[7] in order to justify their position. Again, when presented with the *actual words* from the text they're naming as their full authority, they begin to squirm and become angry and look for loopholes. And when further reminded that Jesus himself was a dark-skinned, homeless refugee—they usually depart the conversation and go back to preaching to the choir of Bible-believing Christians who agree with their selective exegesis.

I'm not having these confrontational conversations to create some sort of *gotcha* moments. I'm reminding people that to one degree or another all Christians create a personal, redacted Bible. I'm showing them that we can't simply *believe* or *not believe* the totality of Scripture. It's intellectually dishonest. We all have to sift through it and interpret it and try to apply it as best we can on a moment-by-moment basis, given what we learn and what we experience. When I'm presented with biblical examples of a violent and vengeful God and confronted with my *own* tendencies to cherry-pick from the Bible, I don't feel the need to deny their existence or run from those passages. I acknowledge that those alternative traits and less desirable images are there and admit the tensions they create in me. I cop to my inconsistency in selectively choosing from the Bible, and I do my best to find ways of letting uncomfortable verses expand my understanding. And ultimately, after all that, I return to the question, "Is this passage consistent with the character of a God who is infinite love?" and I rest in the conclusion I come to.

The Bible is *not* a book. It is a sprawling library of sixty-six separate books, written over thousands of years in multiple languages by dozens of authors, many of unknown origin. The writings range from the vivid poetry of the Genesis creation accounts, to the epic historic stories of the people of Israel, to the intimate worship songs of the Psalms, to the four overlapping yet distinct biographies of Jesus in the Gospels, to the pastoral letters of Paul written to churches in Rome and elsewhere, to the grand apocalyptic visions of Revelation. To say that one *believes* every word of these disparate works, or that one somehow adheres to everything contained in them equally, is at best an impossibility and at worst a convenient lie designed to make someone else feel morally inferior.

I love the Bible. I've studied it for twenty years and shared it with thousands of people—and it's because I love it and because I've studied it that I would never dare to claim that I'm "Bible believing," because the phrase isn't helpful or honest or complex enough for the subject matter. There's a legendary platitude that professed Bible-believing Christians offer in the face of any sustained disagreement, pushback, or challenge, whenever an impasse has been reached: *God said it, I believe it, and that settles it.* That sounds nice and seems appropriately reverent, but it's an oversimplification and it really doesn't mean anything from a practical standpoint, particularly when God is quoted as saying quite a variety of things in Scripture. I think we can do better. I think we can be honest. I think we can instead say to people: *Based on what I've read, these words, translated from ancient manuscripts and assembled thousands of years ago, appear to say this. Sometimes I think God said it and other times I'm not so sure. Through study and prayer and reflection, I'm trying to make some sense out of it, and I'm not certain how it aligns with things written in another part of it, and that bothers me—but maybe we can talk about it.*

FOCUSING ON THE CHARACTER OF GOD

A COMPASSIONATE READING OF SCRIPTURE

I think that kind of admission would be disarming for those on the other sides of our debates and lay fertile ground for us to have redemptive conversations about this faith of ours with those both inside and outside of it. The Bible isn't a textbook. It isn't a formula. It is a complex, spacious, mysterious, sometimes nebulous collection of stories that we are invited to explore as we seek to understand this life and the life beyond it. It requires faith and wonder and digging and discernment, and peace with paradox and comfort with unknowns. We who aspire to be people of the text would likely be much more loving if we could admit that we are Bible reading, we are Bible studying, we are Bible excavating, we are Bible loving—and at some times and with some verses and in some ways and toward some people, we are Bible believing. The less tempted we are to weaponize the words against other people, the more likely we are to find a faith that does no harm. If we use it to make us better humans, that would make us wise stewards of those words. The Good Book makes a really lousy hammer.

Chapter 11

GODFUNDME

I know many people fortunate enough to know God personally. They're able to say with great confidence and specificity what the Maker of All Things is doing at any given moment and His motives, methods, and intentions—especially in times of tragedy and consequence. I used to be one of those people. I used to toss words around lazily, ascribing purpose to the terrible seasons and painful circumstances people pass through. It wasn't done with malice or with an intent to mislead people; I'd just convinced myself that I could make sense of senseless things—because, *Jesus.* Every national disaster, every personal loss, every dire circumstance was space to reiterate my steadfast assurance that God was *in control.* I was hoping to inspire awe and encourage faithfulness, never realizing that this line of thinking also implied that God was causing people those traumas to begin with. I try really hard not to do that anymore. It's been sobering during 2020 to watch religious insiders try to tell the *unenlightened* what God is doing in a pandemic that has killed millions of human beings and shut down the planet, but it's hardly a new phenomenon.

When a series of devastating hurricanes struck in September 2017, sitcom actor turned evangelical celebrity Kirk Cameron took to social media to remind us that the series of massive hurricanes that was leveling large swaths of the planet was just God trying to tell us something. In a video recorded at the Orlando Airport (on his way out of the area, by the way), Cameron sermonized:

> When [God] puts his power on display, it's never without reason. There's a purpose. And we may not always understand what that purpose is, but we know it's not random and we know that weather is sent to cause us to respond to God in humility, awe and repentance.[1]

The storms were not random, he said, they were on purpose—*God's* purpose. They were intentional creations. Never mind that scores of people had been killed, hundreds of thousands left homeless, and many—in the very moments he'd shared the video—endured unimaginable fear and loss. Kirk wanted us all to know that *God* did this to us—and we needed to figure out why.

For decades politicians, celebrities, TV evangelists, and Bible Belt pastors have appointed themselves sanctified meteorologists, telling us why a loving but angry God is pummeling His children with tsunamis, tornadoes, and floods. They've blamed Hollywood and the abortionists and the gays and the Democrats for the Creator of the Universe dialing up some funnel clouds and tidal waves and tearing up the place a bit—so you'll want to repent from whatever it is you did that pissed Him off. (Yes, otherwise innocent people are being devastated in the process of punishing a small segment of the population who won't know they're being specifically targeted but, hey, God works in mysterious ways, right?) Cameron's variation on this theme was more subtle than some of his more incendiary and heavy-handed preacher friends, but it is just as toxic. It places the burden on individual people to psychoanalyze

God; to somehow discern what He is telling *them specifically* in weather events and terrorist attacks that wreak havoc across miles and traumatize multitudes. Talk about operating above your pay grade: figuring out why deadly storms causing billions of dollars of damage or violent acts against hundreds of people in your town is somehow about *you or someone else.* A non-Christian friend commenting on Cameron's video said to me: "So, according to conservatives, this year God elected Trump, killed a girl in Charlottesville, and destroyed hundreds of thousands of homes? He sounds like a real a**hole." Before I could reply, he continued. "And I'm supposed to believe he loves me—why?" My friend, like many people, sees people like Kirk Cameron or Jerry Falwell or Joel Osteen and is certain he wants no part of that kind of malignant, retributive religion. I don't blame them. I don't want any part of it either.

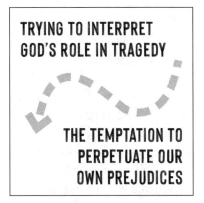

TRYING TO INTERPRET GOD'S ROLE IN TRAGEDY

THE TEMPTATION TO PERPETUATE OUR OWN PREJUDICES

In his first Sunday preaching after the devastation in Houston following Hurricane Harvey, Osteen said to his megachurch congregation (which now included many new refugees), "The reason it may seem like God is not waking up is not because he's ignoring you, not because he's uninterested; it's because he knows you can handle it." So, in a slightly less punitive take (Joel claims), God loves and respects these folks' strength so much that he displaced them, destroyed their belongings and pets, and killed their neighbors. (A pat on the back or a new car would have been sufficient.)

I'm not sure that's a God I'm interested in, and I know it isn't a God that non-Christians will be compelled to seek: one who sounds like an abusive parent or violent partner or family member saying, "I hurt you because I love you."

For all sorts of reasons, it's really precarious business trying to use any painful or deadly events as a platform to preach. First among them: If we're being honest with ourselves, we really have no idea exactly what God does or doesn't do, and just how God works in and around and through weather patterns and mass shootings and widespread tragedies. In the absence of certainty, we should probably choose silence. Second, people who are wounded and grieving and heartbroken need to be cared for, comforted, and embraced—they don't need any armchair theology about why their injury is actually a good thing, or how it's a hidden personal message from the Divine. It's one thing for someone going through difficult circumstances to seek and speculate on such things for themselves, but something else for us to do it for them. Third, and perhaps most importantly, by trying to theologically interpret natural disasters and terrible circumstances, we easily convert tragic events into a sort of weaponized religious propaganda; we end up assigning to God all our fears and prejudices and hang-ups, potentially believing and making other people believe that God is as much of a jerk as we are. I can barely figure out how my microwave works, let alone determine how a catastrophic weather event is being wielded by God to teach you or me or gay couples a lesson, one that if He were God He could easily speak loudly and clearly enough to hear. I would feel like a reckless fraud pretending I know what's happening.

It's ironic that Cameron referred to the book of Job in his video sermon. When Job loses everything and is understandably grief-stricken, at first his friends show wisdom by simply sitting silently with him in his despair, offering their quiet, reassuring presence. Only later do they slowly fall into the familiar temptation of placing blame, interpreting circumstances, and playing God. That's when everything goes sideways: when they move from sympathetic companions to Divine interpreters. Maybe we who claim faith should refrain from pretending we understand how and why pain and suffering befall us. Maybe we should admit the mystery, the discomfort, and the tensions that spirituality yields in terrifying times. Perhaps, when people are being terrorized by nature or by the inhumanity around them, instead of shouting sermons at them, we should simply try to be a loving, compassionate presence that reminds them they aren't alone: a theology of availability, a ministry of showing up and shutting up. If the God you're following and preaching to people in their times of pain is indeed an a-hole—it's probably not God at all. It's probably just you.

Just as the way that we think about pain says a good deal about how we think about God, so does the way we think about prayer. Today, I received an email report from the friend of a man who has spent the past twelve months receiving chemotherapy and radiation in his battle with an aggressive form of throat cancer. After sharing the welcome news of the cancer's remission and the man's recovery, the author added a congratulatory "Our prayers worked!" For years I encountered this sentiment in these kinds of moments without batting an eye, but now they make me slightly nauseous. Now they bring a record-player needle scratch that stops me in my tracks. Now they feel really . . . wrong. There's a scene in the movie *Crimes and Misdemeanors* where character

Cliff Stern looks back on a memory of his large, theologically diverse Jewish family discussing actions and consequences, and his Aunt May says: "There's this joke about the prizefighter who enters the ring. And his brother turns to the family priest and says, 'Father, pray for him.' And the priest said, 'I will. But, if he can punch, it'll help.'"[2] That quote rings true for me in many ways. These days, in the fights for goodness and equity, I pray—but I "punch," too.

PRAYING FOR A PARTICULAR OUTCOME

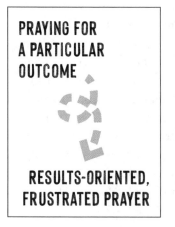

RESULTS-ORIENTED, FRUSTRATED PRAYER

I don't believe prayer works anymore—at least not in the way we people of faith often like to believe it does or claim that it does or how I used to teach that it does. When someone we know or love or read about on social media is gravely ill, we default to asking people to pray for their healing; more specifically, we ask others to ask God to heal them. We enlist people to take our cause (this sick person or dire situation) to the Almighty. I have asked for such prayers thousands upon thousands of times over the past two and a half decades. I've solicited my congregations to pray for children in accidents, young mothers with cancer, and teenage gunshot victims. We have held prayer vigils and extended our hands in church services and created online prayer chains and stood circled around ICU bedsides. In countless moments, like the persistent widow in Jesus' parable or the faithful rooftop friends of a sick man,[3] I have privately and desperately petitioned God to bring miraculous cures, to reverse seemingly hopeless situations, to circumvent dire diagnoses, to move in a particular moment and a particular person. I not only believed that healing was possible—I also believed that I could somehow sway God with words and numbers and fervor to bring it. I don't believe that any longer.

I understand why we do this. Interceding in prayer for other people is a beautiful expression of care and solidarity, an effort to somehow stand beside someone in unthinkable trauma, to let them know that we love them and feel their urgency. In this way, prayer surely works. It lets people understand the depth of our concern for them, allowing them to feel a little less alone, lifting them emotionally and physically as they face the senseless suffering of this life. We should pray and let people know that we are praying for them, that we are pulling for them and thinking of them and standing with them from where we are. I believe prayer changes our hearts as we pray, that it binds us to one another, and that it increases hope in otherwise hopeless situations—but I'm not sure it actually works to save sick people from death. It might not be a good thing if it did.

To contend that God heals when we pray for those who are terribly sick or physically injured or emotionally traumatized is to imagine a Creator who needs to be convinced. It is to paint an image of a God who—though already fully aware of the gravity of the situation and the worry of loved ones and the reality of the injury—refuses to move until we ask Him to. In this way, prayer appeals can almost become spiritual GoFundMe campaigns, where we're told that if we "just get enough people praying," healing will happen, as if there is some unknown magic number or critical mass that will move the Almighty in our favor. We feel the pressure to adequately make our case that a newborn baby or a teenager with cancer or a grandfather in a coma should get a reprieve. By seeing healing as a divine choice, we are essentially praying to change God's mind, asking Him to save people from Himself by undoing suffering He either allowed or manufactured to begin with. The challenging fallout from praying for someone in that way is that we have to make sense of the results afterward. If the person lives or gets better, we somehow believe we have engineered their survival and (if we're cognizant enough of others' suffering) need to process why *our* prayers were enough and those for the person in the next hospital room weren't. And when healing *doesn't* come, we are stuck second-guessing whether we prayed hard enough or lamenting that we didn't enlist enough "prayer warriors" to effectively move God, or we try to figure out why our petitions failed. Either way, it's not a healthy way to engage with the mystical source of all life or the unpredictability of healing and recovery.

I know well the Old Testament Bible stories of divinely delivered floods and plagues and pharaohs, I've read the psalmists' laments about the God who moves in fierce storms and grave sickness, and I'm familiar with Jesus' parables of kings and slave masters punishing subjects and servants for their failures—and I still can't bring myself to declare that any God who is worthy of being God would cause pain in order to reach humanity or withhold recovery to teach them a lesson. What kind of statement are we making about the character of a God whose work can be crowdsourced—and what message are we sending to the loved ones and supporters of sick people who don't get well, who ultimately expire from their illnesses and injuries? Were their prayers not passionate or earnest or frequent enough to nudge God to respond? Did the prayers of a man who didn't survive "not work," and if not, why not? (You rarely see a field-goal kicker kiss a cross or point to the heavens when he misses a kick.) A cause-and-effect theology of prayer makes God far too human. There are times when I reflexively fall back into these efforts to move the Almighty: when people I love face trials and sickness, when the world feels out of my control, when grief overtakes me. In those painful moments of emotional urgency, I again become the wounded beggar pleading with God to fix whatever feels broken—but I quickly realize this is the old muscle memory of my former faith kicking in, and I'm aware that my petitions are a paradox. When I do find myself habitually returning to the posture of imploring God to act, I try to redirect my prayers because I want to move myself more than I try to move God.

Recently, we lost a dear family member at the age of twenty-three. He was a compassionate, kind, funny, brilliant young man who suffered much of his life with a host of autoimmune maladies. He became sick, deteriorated quickly, and passed after only a week. He was loved by hundreds of people who gathered to remember him a few days later; his life touched countless others, and the ripples of this life were changing the world when he became ill. I prayed for him. An army of relatives, friends, and strangers prayed for him. He didn't get better. We all wanted him to. He didn't. I refuse to try to figure out what that says about God's character or about the effectiveness or earnestness of our prayers, because that feels like a fruitless search and it isn't a good use of my grieving. His loss is simply tragic and devastating as a reality, and that's enough. It's enough to agree as his father said via text not long after, "This sucks." The only helpful remaining questions are "Now that this has happened, how will I respond? How will I be changed by it? What will I do now that it's gone so very wrong?" That is the only way loss can be transformed into love, the only truly productive prayer.

I still ask for people to pray and I still pray, but I try to reorient my prayers these days. I no longer believe in a supernatural Santa Claus who dispenses life and death based on the conduct or the heart of the recipients and their friends. I don't believe in a God who withholds miraculous healing or compassionate care until sufficiently begged by us to do so. I believe prayer works by unlocking our empathy for others, that it knits us together in deeper relationship. I believe it to be a beautiful expression of love for and solidarity with people who are suffering; that it connects us personally to one another and to God in ways that cannot be quantified. I believe it is a sacred act of kindness we extend to other human beings to declare oneness with them. But I don't believe prayer can change God's mind about healing people we love—nor do I want it to.

The turbulence of a pandemic-addled year didn't create this toxic theology of prayer, but it certainly has vividly revealed it. Yesterday, I read the social media post of a well-known Christian musician, assuring us that the pandemic that has been decimating the planet is "all part of God's plan." He was prescribing optimism, saying that the Almighty is engineering these days as a way of bringing humankind closer to Him. I may be a really lousy Christian, but I don't think God works that way—at least I really hope not. I think that would make God incredibly cruel and strangely perverse. I don't have any inside information, but my hunch is that an all-powerful, all-knowing creator, who is supposedly made of love, isn't engineering this wide-scale suffering to make a point. I don't believe "God's plan" is for millions of people to be sick and hundreds of thousands dead; for tens of millions of Americans to lose their jobs and hundreds of millions to be at the brink of financial and emotional collapse. I don't believe "God's plan" is distraught human beings having to say good-bye to their parents and spouses and best friends via phone screens or pressed up against the cold glass of an ICU window, or to have to postpone for months grieving together with those they love. I don't believe "God's plan" is a massive isolation that is driving so many to depression and despondency, or bitter national enmity over whether to work and get sick or stay home and go broke, or mental breakdowns caused by the weight of so many swirling stresses and questions.

FOCUSING ON COMPASSIONATE HUMAN RESPONSE TO CRISIS

HOPE IN THE MIDST OF TRIAL

In days when we are gripped so fiercely by fear and worry, experiencing such lack and loneliness, and encountering such oppressive and prevalent grief, all people (but especially people of faith) look for evidence that something else is happening, that there is some purpose to our pain. Religion often wants this purpose to be "God's plan." It doesn't offer any reasons, and it generally creates more questions than it answers, but in a brief moment it feels sufficient. To assume this is God's doing is to declare that though God could work in infinite ways to show us our commonalities and inspire us to faithfulness and allow us to tap into our reservoirs of empathy and courage, God chooses to make millions of people very ill and kill many others to do that.

I am still a person of faith, though that faith is much messier than it used to be. I still believe in something greater that *began the beginning* and that holds this all together, but I try not to decode the intricate puzzle of the excruciating and confounding *whys* of this life in order to discover God. I don't try to make sense of senseless things. Instead, I look for God in the way that human beings respond when those senseless things happen: when people die too young, when natural disasters come, when pervasive sickness spreads. Instead of spending too much time and bandwidth interpreting the *reason* such things happen, I watch for the better angels here on the ground: the helpers and the healers and the caregivers and the embracers—and I find meaning there. I try to unearth something more gentle or courageous or grateful in response. So, rather than God's *plan,* which is much too difficult to see from the street level, I look for God's *presence:* for the compassion and mercy and love and goodness that feel like whatever God is supposed to feel like.

I have seen that presence in the bruises around the eyes of nurses who've slept in hospital supply closets. I've seen it in the creativity of schoolteachers, needing to transform their curricula and teaching styles in a matter of weeks. I have heard God in musicians singing on their high-rise balconies to sleepless cities starved for songs of hope. I see God in strangers anonymously dropping off diapers and toilet paper and rice in neighbors' mailboxes; in the small acts of kindness and benevolence that remind people who feel unloved of their belovedness, that make isolated people feel less alone, that offer some measure of healing to broken bodies, that bring a moment of peace to assailed minds. Again, I may be wrong, but I don't believe that whatever or whoever God is, such devastation and death are part of that

God's plan. The best guess I have right now is that this season of suffering we've recently experienced together in the pandemic (like all moments) is the sacred space for those of us who claim faith to live what we believe: to persevere and to give and to heal—and above all, to love. That love is the only plan, and incarnating it here is the greatest prayer.

Chapter 12

INSIDE JOB

There's a scene from a horror movie from my childhood titled *When A Stranger Calls* that's never left me. A teenager is babysitting some kids in the neighborhood. After they're asleep, the babysitter receives a series of phone calls from a strange man. His interruptions gradually become more frequent and more and more threatening, and after repeatedly telling him to leave her alone, she finally calls the police and (this being in the days before caller ID) asks them to trace the source of the call. The phone soon rings again and as the woman attempts to shout down what she expects is her anonymous tormentor, she hears the panic-stricken voice of the officer on the other end of the line, giving her the heart-stopping news: the call is coming from inside the house! The idea of imminent danger being *that* close and the shock of that moment absolutely terrified me. I'm not sure I've ever been the same since then. I'm fifty-one and when I'm at home by myself, I still turn on all of the lights—and the TV—and the dryer, for some reason.

That's the true story of religion in America. As someone who has made their home and livelihood inside organized Christianity, the most sobering realization in recent years as we have grown more divided and outwardly angry as a nation is that the greatest assault on the faith of my childhood and on vulnerable people around me seems like an inside job. While we religious people tend to look at external causes for decline in church attendance (changing social habits, a secularization of the culture, watered-down theology, the "gay agenda") we often have a difficult time looking in the mirror. If we were to reflect and have honest conversations with one another—and more importantly, with people outside our gatherings—we'd likely find that the most serious wounds to the body of Christ have been self-inflicted. The Church is not fighting the rebellious, faithless, heathen world, as I'd always been taught, but itself. And as a result, I find myself in two fierce battles lately. I am simultaneously fighting both *with* and *for* my faith tradition. Some days I'm working passionately to convince disillusioned people to stay there because I want them to experience the beauty that I have seen firsthand; other days I'm telling them to run, as if Godzilla is about to squash them, because I know how much destruction it is causing, the way it is preying upon vulnerable people, the corrupt power it wields against the already marginalized.

You've probably seen the ubiquitous meme floating around, or at one point or another you've posted or expressed the thought contained in it: *I Can't Adult Today.* It's the idea that whatever it is that is required of proper, responsible, grown-up human beings, one is simply not presently capable of it. For whatever reason, that day, the task of *adulting* seems impossible. I've been a Christian for most of my fifty-one years, a pastor in the local church for more than half of them. And on far too many mornings recently, I've woken up, checked Twitter or watched the news or walked away from family conversations or departed church gatherings, and thought to myself: "I can't Christian today." I can no longer be tethered to this thing that is so toxic and so painful to so many. I can't wade through any more bad theology and predatory behavior from pulpit-pounding pastors who seem solely burdened to exclude and to wound and to do harm. I can't sift through all this malice and bitterness masquerading as Christianity to try to find what of it is left worth keeping. I can't do any more face-palming while reading another celebrity evangelist's tweets about walls at the border or seeing the viral video of joyless people spewing racist rants at fast-food restaurants—all while saying they follow the same Jesus I do. I can't apologize anymore for people who are willfully hurting other human beings in the name of a God they preach is love. I can't align myself with the human rights violations and overt racism and rabid nationalism that is defining Christianity in America. If being a Christian now means such things—count me out. You can keep that religion.

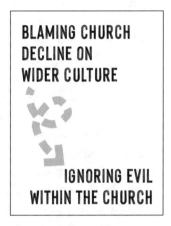

BLAMING CHURCH DECLINE ON WIDER CULTURE

IGNORING EVIL WITHIN THE CHURCH

Maybe you're a Christian or a former Christian who understands this exasperation. Maybe you've experienced having a thing you once felt at home in suddenly feel like foreign soil, a religious worldview that was solid bedrock gradually begin to shake, stuff that you knew that you knew that you knew with all your being become something you're no longer certain of at all. You might be living in the tension of being associated with something that you now suspect may be causing more harm than good and wondering whether to stay and change it or defect for a new homeland. I understand. Given this, I find myself asking a question that I like to ask of similarly frustrated followers of Jesus: "Is Christianity helpful anymore?" Not is it true or real or provable or noble—is it helpful? Is its net effect on humanity redemptive? Is it marked mostly by love or by something else? As we seek to be agents of compassion in the world, and as we interact with more people who know the Jesus story only through Franklin Graham and alt-right Proud Boys and discriminatory bathroom bills and Muslim bans— is claiming this faith now a liability to authentic relationships because of the unscalable barrier it represents? Is the name *Christian* now so inextricably entwined with misogyny, bigotry, and homophobia that it cannot be untangled? Now that it has been so politicized and weaponized by a political party for its own gain, can we ever hope to reclaim it? Have we lost the battle for the name of Jesus to the wall builders and the transphobes and the white supremacists? The answers don't seem encouraging.

At a small house gathering in Tulsa prior to a speaking event there, a tearful woman approached me and shared the story of the painful decision to leave her longtime church after its stance on immigration and response to the Black Lives Matter protests proved irreconcilable to her, given her understanding of the life and ministry of Jesus. She'd served on several committees while there, had spearheaded social programs, and challenged church leaders to be more explicit on justice issues—but ultimately, she couldn't make peace with the slow rate of movement and the silence in days she wanted the community to speak. "I feel like I lost," she said, "like maybe I gave up too soon, like maybe I should have stayed and changed the church." "You *have* changed the church," I said. "You left it." I reminded her that she had renovated that specific congregation during those years by her presence—and that she was still altering it through her absence, and that both were honorable. I assured her that not only was her former church collectively nudged toward equity and diversity due to her being there for all that time, but her departure might serve as a catalyst for decisions that might never otherwise be made. (She may have been the "final straw" of human attrition, causing leaders to wake up.) I encouraged her that she was creating an entirely new community now that she could be a more authentic version of herself, whether she called that church or not. She agreed, but all those things didn't lessen the sense of loss she felt.

Though it is a fairly tenuous connection these days, I am still tethered to my religious tradition by a combination of present personal conviction along with the spiritual muscle memory of my past—and right now it honestly feels like more the latter than the former. There is an attrition to my joy lately when I consider the company the word *Christian* places me in. I find it more and more difficult with each passing day to outwardly claim this faith because of what that declaration now immediately aligns me with in the eyes of the watching world. It aligns me with homophobic politicians and Muslim-hating celebrity evangelists and perpetually oppressed seasonal Christmas warriors; with gun-toting preachers and damnation-wielding social media trolls and predatory presidents. It now aligns me with the least-like-Jesus stuff I can imagine and, honestly, that grieves me. To some people, this is all Christianity is—and therefore that is what defines me and all other professed Christians in their eyes. These people believe they know me: my politics, passions, and convictions. They think they know how I feel about gay marriage and immigrants and women's rights. They don't realize that I am sickened by this thing claiming to be Christianity, too. They don't know that I am as burdened as they are to resist its toxins. They don't know that I am in this turbulence alongside them. They don't see that I totally get that this monstrosity claiming to be of Jesus would be unrecognizable to him—that he would be as horrified by it as they are and I am. Seeing the loud and angry religion that often has the microphone, I want to be a stark dissenting opinion. I want the expression of my faith to make them at least think twice.

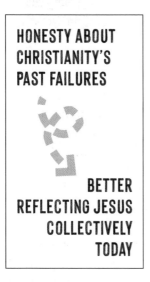

HONESTY ABOUT CHRISTIANITY'S PAST FAILURES

BETTER REFLECTING JESUS COLLECTIVELY TODAY

Sometimes, I'm not sure why anyone would choose Christianity if they weren't already a Christian. I love my faith tradition. I can't have a different origin story than I have. Yet, as meaningful as it has been and still often is, I'm cognizant of the fact that it was my spiritual inheritance: the story of God given to me on arrival by the people who raised me. If I'd entered into the world at any other place and time, to any other family, I'd have a completely different story. God wouldn't have changed, of course—but everything about the way I see, describe, and understand this unaltered God would be profoundly altered. That truth allows me to breathe when I feel the pressure to stay in my old story becomes suffocating: God is outside the story, too. God is beyond my building.

This may feel like an uncomfortable drift toward universalism, and in the best ways I imagine you're right. It isn't that what you believe doesn't matter, it's that the object of your belief is not bound by those things. If we are people of faith, our religious traditions loom large for each of us. I know that in many ways that I'll never be able to fully identify, I am still a Christian because I have always *been* a Christian: because I know what I know about Jesus, and I can see when people are stealing his identity and bastardizing his legacy. I know when they're twisting the Scriptures to subjugate people, when they're fashioning God in their own terrified image, when they're slapping a veneer of religiosity on something with no redemptive value. Because I've experienced the authentic treasure of diverse, loving community, I know when a counterfeit Christ is being sold by people brokering in bigotry. I'm able to see the frauds and the false prophets because I've experienced the real and the beautiful of this faith—but not everyone has, and so I don't blame them for rejecting it all. It is often completely rejectable. Jesus spent a good deal of his life acknowledging this same injurious religious movement, and so their objections make sense to me. If all I had to go on was this malicious, power-hungry, bullying, bitter thing I see running amok every day in America, I'd run from it too. If following Jesus meant signing up for all of this, I'd have no interest either. Sadly, the American Church has in many ways become the greatest argument for someone not becoming a Christian, for rejecting organized religion and never looking back.

If that was all there was to this faith, I'd opt out of it too—but I know better. I know that there are other expressions of Christianity here, though they may not have the megaphones and megachurches and social media bandwidth. There are inclusive, redemptive communities filled with people of empathy and generosity and mercy; human beings who are earnestly striving to emulate Jesus and who are rightly embarrassed by the hatred perpetuated in his name, who believe in loving their neighbor as themselves and welcoming the outsider and outcast, who believe the table is open to anyone who comes hungry, and who believe compassion is our highest aspiration. There are millions of Christians who reject the very intolerance those now outside local church communities reject, who are sickened by the same hypocrisy they are sickened by, who condemn the violence they condemn, who deeply grieve over the hatred they grieve over. If you've made your exodus from organized religion, maybe these things aren't enough for you to reconsider, but hopefully it will be enough to let you know that people are standing with you, that many of us who claim faith in Jesus have no interest in this kind of Christianity because we know Jesus wouldn't either. When people in the Gospels were pushed to the periphery by unloving religious people, they usually ended up closer to Jesus.

Not long ago, I was having a Twitter exchange with a woman who identified as a queer agnostic of color. She was lamenting the way she feels that Bible Belt evangelicals have sold their souls and thrown their support behind unapologetically racist political candidates, the way they've bullied sexual assault survivors and demonized immigrants and made an idol of the flag. I implored her, "Don't be swayed by this! This violent, perverse thing isn't Christianity!" She replied, "Actually John, it *is* Christianity. By and large, this has been my experience of Christians. This is the rule: all this venom and fearmongering and sexism. People like you are the exception. People like you are the outliers. People like you are the strange ones." She said, "Your heresy is why I love you!" In other words, the idea of an empathetic Christian seems like an oxymoron to her, an aberration that deviates wildly from the norm.

Part of perpetuating a more loving expression of the faith tradition of Jesus is reckoning with the reality that so much of it is a liability, as we engage a world increasingly suspicious of those who share our namesake. I suspect my social media acquaintance speaks for many people. More than ever, Christianity is synonymous with discrimination and exclusion, which means openhearted, equality-loving, diversity-welcoming followers of Jesus may need to make a difficult choice. We may need to, in some ways, secede from this thing in order to fully live it out. We may need to lose our status as *Christians in good standing* in order to hold on to our souls and to reveal a Jesus who has been concealed in the system itself.

People tell me things. It is one of the great treasures of this work. When I meet strangers who've read my writing, they often feel safe to share what they may not be able to tell anyone else—sometimes almost immediately. Elsa was one of those people. A couple of months ago we met following a speaking event at a local church, and after some brief and unassuming small talk, her voice quivered as she began to tell me about a devastating season in her life: loss and grief and helplessness of a kind I'll never comprehend—or at least hope I won't. Her story leveled me. I did the best I could to let her know that she was seen and heard, and I tried to encourage her as I was able in those few moments, surrounded by hundreds of people who had no idea of the gravity of our conversation or the scalding pain and disorienting panic she was in. As our time was coming to a close, Elsa asked for a hug and I gladly obliged. She wiped away the tears that had pooled in her eyes and had begun spilling onto her cheeks, smiled bravely, and said, "Being human is hard. Thank you for helping make it not so hard for me," and walked away.

Elsa is right: being human is hard. We weren't prepared for it. None of us asked to be here, and we didn't have any choice about when and where we arrived, the kind of people who would welcome and shape us, or most of what happened for the first two decades of our lives. And even after that, we never really have control over very much, despite sometimes imagining that we do. We come wired for all sorts of fears and worries and phobias, we're saddled with individual quirks and idiosyncrasies that so easily derail our progress, and we have persistent voices in our heads that criticize and condemn and can be nearly impossible to turn off. And when we step out of our heads and into the world, we expose ourselves to unthinkable suffering there too. People we let close to us sometimes damage us and do us harm. Strangers purposefully and unintentionally do us damage. We lose those we love in brutal, senseless, excruciating ways. Despite our best plans and preparations and intentions, things sometimes fall apart. We wrestle continually with unanswerable questions about the hows and whys of our existence. Like Elsa, we all need something that makes the weight bearable, that makes the pains endurable, that makes us feel less alone, that lets the radiant light of hope stream in through the window blinds—something that helps make being human not so hard.

ERRING TOWARD KINDNESS

A MORE LOVING RELIGION

Honestly, I don't know if organized Christianity, on balance, is helpful anymore. What I *do* know is that the compassionate heart of Jesus I find in the stories told about him *is* helpful—and urgently needed. The world can use more tenderhearted humans, doing what they can to live selflessly, gently, and focused on others—and that's probably the highest spiritual aspiration we can have: leaving people more loved than we found them. I want to stand with the empathetic souls, no matter where they come from and what they call themselves and who they declare God to be, because that is the most pressing need I see in the world. I want to be with the disparate multitude who believe caring for others is the better path, even if that means never stepping foot in a church building again or doing the hard work of renovating the ones we're connected to. People who are assailed by the storms of this life don't need any more heartless, loveless, joyless self-identified saints claiming they're Christian while beating the hell out of them. They need people who simply give a damn in a way that emulates Jesus, people who see how hard it is to be human and feel burdened to make it a little softer. When I leave this place, I'm not very interested that anyone declares me appropriately religious or properly Christian. I'd rather have them say that to the marginalized and alone and hurting and invisible, to the weary, wounded, tired people around me in this life—I was helpful. That's something within my control. That's the inside job that matters.

Chapter 13
A SEMI-PRO-LIFE MOVEMENT

I find that I cuss a lot lately. I'm not taking about an infrequent verbal indiscretion, but a steady and prolific, George Carlin–level, freestyle flow of expletives. I'm not particularly proud of this revelation but I'm also not apologizing for it, either. After a few months of persistent, low-grade guilt, I've since come to the conclusion that given the far less than ideal conditions (an extended quarantine with two self-employed parents, two kids doing online schooling, and two dogs both living their best lives), if dropping a few well-timed, cathartic f-bombs into the ether helps me find a little mental equilibrium in the dizzying tumult of an unprecedented planetary disaster—that's a relatively acceptable trade-off. This unvarnished part of me isn't pretty but it's honest, and I'm comfortable with this pairing: *ugly authenticity*. Come to think of it, the best kind of religion works that way: truthful, even if a little less than pretty. It's a shame so many of us place so much energy into maintaining a beautiful lie, when a God who is actually love would make that pretending unnecessary and rather heretical.

When we lose our filters and facades (whether by choice or merely for survival), the truer versions of ourselves show up and—depending on what that reveals and who's watching—the results can be glorious or tragic, the change welcome or disheartening. Having said that, truth comes with a cost. Over the past couple of years, encountering so many unfiltered, professed Christians has been a source of profound grieving for me. I am seeing many people for the first time, and it isn't pleasant. You learn a lot about other people and about yourself in a pandemic. An extended daily diet of forced isolation, sustained urgency, perceived helplessness, and abject terror tends to take away any pretense and reveal the less flattering parts of ourselves: the parts we're usually able to allocate enough energy to in order to keep hidden. Under normal conditions, a thin veneer of decorum and a bit of ornamental religiosity can cover a multitude of sins for long periods of time, but wholesale, cataclysmic trauma like we've experienced in the path of COVID-19 doesn't allow for such expendable emotional income. In days when flights are grounded and shelves are barren and schools are shut down and our margins are thin, we need those precious resources just to survive, and some decorative pursuits fall away. We become a little bit more of who we are at our core—which is why they say that crises don't create character but simply reveal it.

One recent morning, I noticed a social media post from an old friend from my former church. We lost touch a couple of years ago, and seeing her name on my timeline immediately caught my attention. I soon wished it hadn't. She'd penned a venomous tirade expressing outrage at being "forced" to wear a mask at the grocery store: claiming personal persecution, chastising our Democratic governor, condemning the Liberal Media, publicly condemning the local grocery store manager—and defiantly refusing to use a face covering on the grounds that "God would protect" her. (She made no mention of other people, or of the fact that God had to this date not "protected" around 7.8 million Americans.) In a closing stream of scalding non

sequiturs, she also complained about the Black Lives Matter movement and the "looters" who deserved the rubber
bullets that they'd gotten from heavily armed federal troops
in Portland the night before. Had my friend's name and
thumbnail portrait not appeared above this bitter, rant-
ing manifesto, I'd have never identified her as the author
or suspected she'd be capable of such callousness. This is
the same woman who'd proudly worn her "pro-life" convictions on both her sleeve and rear
bumper for as long as I'd known her.
The cognitive dissonance of seeing
her passionate protest *against* masks
in the throes of a deadly public
health crisis and her malice toward
those protesting police brutality was
profound—though probably not as
jarring to my system as it might have
been if it were not such a common
experience: facing the hypocrisy of
professed pro-life Christians who
show disregard for so much of the
life on this planet.

A FIXATION ON ABORTION

A NARROW UNDERSTANDING OF LIFE

It's difficult for people outside
of organized Christianity to fathom how so many believers
reconcile this prevalent inconsistency or justify such fierce
loyalty to a politician or party with such contempt for so
many iterations of humanity—all in the name of protecting
human life. The abortion issue has been named by millions
of self-identified religious people as their moral deal breaker,
their hard line in the sand, their singular hill to die on—but
their lack of a consistent pro-life ethic regarding diverse sentient human beings who have already exited the birth canal
is something that a generation of faithful, once-faithful, and

faithless people alike cannot make sense of or peace with. They rightly cannot reconcile how so many followers of Jesus are seemingly able to place the word "abortion" on one side of a massive moral scale—and have it far outweigh the lives of caged children, mass shooting victims, murdered Black men; or the prevalent threats of generational poverty, systemic racism, and a litany of human rights atrocities that barely seem to register or matter.

There are a number of explanations for this highly selective zealotry by religious people but ultimately, I think it comes down to laziness and self-preservation. I think embryos are relatively easy to advocate for. They don't encroach upon people's privilege or confront their politics or challenge their theology or require much from them in the way of lifestyle change. It is a clean form of activism, certainly far less messy and uncomfortable than having to defend people you don't like or that you've declared the enemy, or people you are afraid of because you've been conditioned to be by your parents, pastors, news channels, and seminary professors. By putting all their eggs (so to speak) into the basket of fervently defending life in utero, religious people can feel the intoxicating, easy high of self-righteousness and moral virtue—without having to actually *love people*: strange, disparate, uncomfortable-for-you-to-be-around people. That's because embryos can be idealized into something pleasant and palatable, devoid of any of the messy characteristics they find undesirable in actual walking-around human beings. They aren't yet gay or Muslim or liberal or Black or poor or atheist (or whatever other qualifiers trouble you), and so affinity with them is uncomplicated, solidarity with them does not cross the lines of their tribalism. Anti-abortion believers get to feel like noble advocates for Life, while still holding onto their prejudices and hang-ups and hatred. They can dispense all kinds of cruelty and expose human beings to staggering forms of bigotry—and still say they're defending the living.

People outside of this theocratic box recognize the problem with such narrow, crusading fervor: once these embryos are no longer embryos, these supposed life-lovers often don't treat them as though they're even human. Nine or thirteen or thirty-two or sixty-five years later, when they show up in their communities and in their emergency rooms and along their borders, in need of food or refuge or health care or compassion—they're no longer something sacred or beautiful. Unless *these* lives conform to the narrowest and most stringent of criteria, they're more often considered threats to be neutralized and adversaries to be destroyed.

Embryos that grow into LGBTQ teenagers aren't worthy of their protection. Instead, they receive their contempt, bear the brunt of their jokes, and absorb the full damnation of their brimstone sermons. They can't get married or use a public bathroom or get benefits for their partners without being assailed at every turn by these "lovers of life." Embryos that become terrified migrants fleeing crime and poverty and pressed up against the most urgent desperation don't merit the passionate defense inside their country they might have received while inside the womb. Instead, they sustain their scorn and suspicion and every bit of their malicious, wall-building bitterness. Embryos that become sick middle-aged adults fighting metastasizing tumors, facing astronomical chemotherapy bills, and desiring medical care that will not drive them to bankruptcy don't elicit a shred of the empathy they'd have garnered when they were still microscopic. Embryos that one day stand in need of government assistance to keep the lights on or food on the table for their children because they have endured unthinkable adversity along their journey will not be met with tearful embraces by these so-called *life-lovers.* They're derided as lazy and irresponsible, told to pull themselves up by their bootstraps, while never having the benefit of boots. Embryos that one day worship in Muslim communities around these white Christians aren't afforded any passionate defense and aren't celebrated with effusive social media soliloquies. They're instead branded as terrorist sympathizers and excluded via travel bans, their religious freedoms ignored and their very existence resented with coldness in the checkout line and side-eye stares in the airport.

Most ironically of all, embryos that grow into women who desire autonomy over their own bodies will find their lives and wills are now of little concern. They will be legislatively subjugated by those who'd have once declared them precious. And the "pro-life" Christians do all of this (they claim) because they believe that embryos are human beings and they want those beloved embryonic human beings to be cherished, defended, and protected at all costs, which all sounds quite admirable if that were the whole story— but it isn't.

Adopting a consistent pro-life ethic regarding health care or poverty or the environment or gun violence or the death penalty is challenging—because it might mean sitting with the hypocrisy of our current conduct toward vulnerable communities. To live with any continuity toward human life would require an empathy that may prove too high a price to pay; it would demand from us an equity that encroaches on our comfort, and it would mean facing the reality of our privilege. Truly coming to a fervent and full defense of life would mean confronting our phobias and fears and biases, and none of us are ever in a hurry to do such things.

At a campaign rally in Panama City Beach, Florida, President Trump was speaking about the supposed crisis of immigrants overrunning US borders when someone in the crowd yelled, "Shoot them!" Trump erupted in a curled Cheshire cat grin, while sarcastically saying, "Only in the panhandle you can get away with that statement, folks."[1] The crowd laughed and roared in approval. Later, they reposted clips on social media in support. These "pro-life Christians" were proud of this moment. These declared defenders of sacred human life were laughing at the suggestion of murder. An incident like this is revelatory because it exposes the duplicity that allows people to be selectively loving, to disregard so much of the humanity in their path.

A CONSISTENT ETHIC OF LIFE

A MORE ROBUST, COMPLEX SPIRITUALITY

I think our faith demands more of us. My lifetime of study, prayer, activism, and reflection has convinced me that the true litmus test for a professed Christian (and for any person of faith, morality, and conscience, for that matter) isn't one particular policy or isolated stated position or any slogan you affix to a podium—it is the answer to a single, elemental question: Do you care about other people? That's the actual *pro-life* measurement. Christians should be pro-life in the truest sense, in that we are *for humanity.* I wish more professed pro-life Christians had the same passion for migrant children, school shooting victims, sick toddlers, young Black men, Muslim families, LGBTQ teens, the environment, and women's equality that they claim to have for embryos. Then they'd actually be fully, not selectively, pro-*life*, and we'd all be able to work together to care for humanity wherever there is need to do so.

Jesus' call to love others challenges us to a wider defense of the living: Do we treasure all life fiercely? Do we advocate for all of it passionately? Do we oppose all legislation that assails it? Are we burdened with it regardless of where it resides? Does our defense of people transcend pigmentation, orientation, nation of origin? Until many Christians find a pro-life ethic that is not bound by politics or preference, we're not going to be able to fully embrace our calling to love all our neighbors, and we're going to continue to put a barrier between the Church and those who think humanity beyond the birth canal matters.

I believe that God is pro-choice—and that the Bible tells us so. If you contend that God exists, and claim the Christian Scriptures to be your primary guide in understanding the character of that God, you find out pretty early on that free will is kind of a big deal to God. The opening chapters of the book of Genesis describe in poetic language God speaking all creation into being, fashioning out of dark and formless chaos every radiant bit of this planet and its inhabitants: all the light, shape, and color of the disparate beauty here. Whether you're a believer or not, you likely know the Genesis chapter 1 story: six days of grand artistry, six days of spectacular displays of creative power, a boatload of animals, two people, and a seventh day of rest in its very goodness (followed by one tree, one piece of fruit, one serpent, and the mess that follows).

We often focus on the fall (the forbidden fruit) in the story, but fail to see that the heart of the creation narrative leading up to it is God giving human beings the right to determine their own path. They are divinely endowed with self-determination. They are co-creators in their own stories. They are not mindless robots or blind sycophants. They get to choose, because God wants them to choose. God doesn't choose for them, other people don't choose for them, and the government doesn't choose for them. Though not a literal account, the first chapter of Genesis presents the Maker of All Things creating every member of humankind inherently good, specifically original, bearing a striking resemblance to God—and able and qualified to decide who they are and how they live and move and breathe through this life. For professed Christians, it is antithetical to God's intentions to attempt to legislatively control a woman's body, because the higher law says that she is in control of it. Period. For professed Christians, this shouldn't be about debating anything but whether or not women should be allowed to have what God has already given them: choice.

BEING MORE THAN A SINGLE-ISSUE CHRISTIAN

SEEKING THE INTERCONNECTEDNESS OF EVERY ISSUE

And for any supposed believer who claims the Bible directs them, arguing against a woman's right to choose is arguing against the very heart of God as depicted in the Scriptures. I am a Christian man and I am pro-life, in the sense that I am *pro* the lives of *women* having autonomy over their own bodies. Beyond that, I yield to what they do with that autonomy, because neither I nor anyone else should have jurisdiction there. Christian, you're entitled to believe that life is sacred. I certainly do. You're entitled to believe that embryos are equivalent to fully-formed, sentient human beings. I disagree with that assessment and we can talk about why. But you're not entitled by any Scripture passage or any biblical mandate to legislatively force your will upon another human being, no matter what justification you make for it. If you want to argue that, you're fully welcome to. You're just going to have to take your agenda above me and above anyone else—to a decidedly pro-choice God.

Chapter 14
HOLY FEROCITY

A family member I hadn't seen in a few years texted me, seemingly out of the blue: "You're coming across as really angry lately," he said.

"Good," I replied immediately. "I was afraid I wasn't communicating clearly."

Not properly appreciating my sarcasm in the spirit in which it was offered, he continued sternly, "I feel sorry for you, for all that anger—especially as a Christian."

"Don't," I said. "I know why I'm angry and I think it's worth it."

Anger tends to get a bad rap in the Church. Granted, it's not among Paul's celebrated "fruits of the Spirit"[1] and it isn't going to make a short list of most people's commonly named characteristics of Jesus—but as we think about love-less religion and hateful Christianity, it's important to clarify that anger and love *aren't* mutually exclusive. In fact, sometimes what looks from the outside like simply the former is actually profoundly prompted by the latter. It is not rage merely for the sake of rage, but for the sake of justice: a holy discontent that internally disrupts us, first to the point of agitation and then to action.

Yes, the spiritual traditions and the great thinkers before us rightly warn against the potential toxicity of unhealthy, cultivated anger. Buddha says, "Holding on to anger is like grasping a hot coal with the intent of throwing it at someone else; you are the one who gets burned." Albert Einstein writes that "anger dwells only in the bosom of fools." Plato cautions, "There are two things a person should never be angry at: what they can help, and what they cannot." And of course, Jesus preached, "But I tell you that if you are angry with a brother or sister, you will be liable to judgment; and if you insult a brother or sister, you will be liable to the council; and if you say, 'You fool,' you will be liable to the hell of fire."[2] As a fairly fiery spirit prone to passionate responses to the world (I'll credit my Italian mother for that gift), this kind of wise consensus against anger, well—it really pisses me off.

The Greek philosopher Aristotle offers a different way of thinking about the redemptive possibilities of our outrage that merits considering: "Anyone can get angry—that is easy—or give or spend money; but to do this to the right person, to the right extent, at the right time, with the right motive, and in the right way, that is not for everyone, nor is it easy."[3] Using these various qualifiers to measure our expression of anger can be game changers whether you're a person of faith or not: the right person—right extent—right time—right motive—right way. So, the *object* of our anger, the *level* of our anger, the *timing* of our anger, the *purpose* of our anger, and the *manner* of our anger, all matter. These *who, how much, when, why, how* questions can give us a really useful filter for assessing the appropriate nature of our outrage, and more importantly, a productive expression of it. (Which *is* inherently spiritual. See: the patriarchs, the prophets, Jesus, the disciples, etc.) It can be difficult to gauge such things, especially when emotion clouds our minds in the moments that we most need clarity. This is because our anger in the immediate present is often about something other than what we imagine it is. (My friend, minister Doug Hammack, refers to it as "the thing under the thing," the idea that when afflictive emotions surface, it's usually not about the present moment and the seemingly obvious source.) For example, when someone you live with doesn't put a dirty glass in the dishwasher and you blow a gasket, it probably isn't about the glass: it may be about you feeling disrespected or not listened to, about being frustrated with your inability to keep the house clean, about the general disorganization of your family—or even far deeper burdens like financial insecurity, existential angst, unresolved relational conflict, emotional disconnection, profound grief—stuff you've been carrying around for decades. The dirty glass on the countertop isn't the dynamite, it's just the current detonator.

But there are times when the thing in front of us *is* the thing: when the obvious sources in the present moment that trigger our outrage are, in fact, the right person and the right time—and we have to decide the right extent, motive, and way to move in response. As spiritual people, that means we invite God or a higher power or our better angels into the initial anger and we let our response be the answer to a prayer we can't even find words for.

ASSESSING THE OBJECT AND PURPOSE OF OUR ANGER

USING ANGER APPROPRIATELY

This week, in the middle of the Black Lives Matter protests, I watched a self-titled Line of Moms in Portland: a group of women who locked arms and stood between protesters and a heavily armored, heavily armed paramilitary presence sent there precisely to provoke and harass and to use force. These mothers were inarguably angry, but their anger was fueled by their love for humanity and by the imminent threat to it; their anger propelled them out of their homes and into these far more treacherous streets. There was nothing hateful or destructive or even hostile in their actions, even if they were being received by the officers as adversarial and being greatly vilified by those opposing the BLM movement. In fact, their defiance felt like a profoundly sacred act simply by being a presence that affirmed humanity. It was holy ground there on the pavement in Portland, and it resembled Jesus as much as any carefully crafted sermon. It turns out, hatred and anger are often in the eyes of the beholder.

Have you ever met an angry person who didn't believe they were right to be angry? Me either. Christians tend to justify themselves with the phrase *righteous anger,* which I'd just as soon jettison, because the truth is, whether you're conservative or progressive, religious or not, everyone believes their anger is righteous, their cause is just, and their motives are pure (I know I usually do). But if there's any kind of anger people of faith, morality, and conscience should aspire to it is *redemptive anger,* focusing on what results from our responses, the fruit of our efforts and our activism: Do they bring justice, equity, wholeness? Are more people heard and seen and respected in their wake? Is diversity nurtured or assailed because of them?

Come to think of it, the word *anger* may be the problem, since it's gotten some pretty bad PR over the past few million years. I suggest that people of faith interested in protecting the common good replace the word *anger* with *ferocity:* the way a family dog fiercely defends a small child from a coyote attack, the way a mother fiercely defends her baby in a fire, the way my wife fiercely defends me when there's a spider in the bathtub. Ferocity for humanity is what birthed the civil rights movement, the women's movement, the fight for LGBTQ equality, the Black Lives Matter movement, propelling people into sacrificial acts of love on behalf of other people. And ferocity for human beings made in the image of God was the fuel for Jesus turning over the tables and calling out the religious leaders and declaring solidarity with the poor and allowing himself to be executed.[4] I think an underappreciated part of Jesus that tends not to get featured in needlepoints and memes is his righteous pissed-offness: his passionate objections to seeing the powerful preying upon the vulnerable, watching the religious hypocrites pollute the system, witnessing the well-fed living close-fisted toward the hungry. You can't have this passionate response to the world without anger as its initial propellant. It is the spiritually combustible ignition point of our activism.

> **INVITING GOD INTO OUR ANGER**
>
> **CHANNELING IT INTO SOMETHING REDEMPTIVE**

And this ferocity for humanity, as necessary and pure as it might be, will often be interpreted negatively by those seeking to do damage to humanity. It will be labeled angry and hateful by people who benefit from inequity and injustice—and religious people on the opposite side of our convictions will sometimes attempt to shame us into silence in the name of the Jesus they probably would have had a real problem with. The beautiful collective outrage of good people is actually the antidote to hateful religion. That *not-rightness* is what bends the arc of the moral universe toward justice.[5] We cannot afford to grow so tired or complacent or apathetic that we lose our ability to be outraged, and we can't be so concerned with decorum that we soften ourselves too much. I think we have to hold on to our intolerance to injustice because it comes from a sacred source that will tether us to other people. When you take a certain medication for a long time, you can eventually build up tolerance to it. It no longer works. We must not build up a tolerance to inhumanity, which is incredibly easy right now because we see so much of it. We are feeling this profound discomfort because we are fiercely defending lives from danger, and people around us are going to experience equal discomfort when we do, which is a challenge for faith communities who prefer everyone getting along, even if they just pretend to.

The events of 2020 interrupted the cycle of curated niceness and conflict avoidance for many churches. The reverberations of the murder of George Floyd and the protests and counter-protests that followed, broke that tenuous truce in many local faith communities and denominations, disrupting the facade of civility and daring to expose the raw wounds and scalding passions of our core beliefs on race. The simple words *Black Lives Matter* became the lumbering elephant in the room of religious white people that simply could no longer be ignored. It's created genuine conflict within communities that were able to sidestep it before, and though invasive, this is a welcome moment. Places where people of faith, morality, and conscience gather should be courageous environments where the absolute most difficult aspects of being human are laid bare. We should be marked by our tough conversations, our awkward silences, and our upended tables. We've inverted church by imagining it should be the most comfortable, most pleasant part of our week: a place where we just feel good feelings and think happy thoughts. I'm not sure that's biblical or helpful or loving, because there are people outside our buildings who don't have that luxury; they're outside breaking their backs for the crumbs of their daily bread, living with urgency as their default setting. As a pastor, sometimes I wanted the people in my care to leave a church service feeling comforted, of course, but just as often I wanted them to be burdened to run from it and into the places where pain is commonplace in order to make them less painful. I think that's what love does. I think real love is fierce and relentless and it risks being misunderstood because of just how passionate it is.

I was leading a leadership retreat at an aging Presbyterian church in North Jersey, just a short bridge away from New York City. We were discussing the reality of a disruptive, social justice Jesus, when a sweet woman from the ministry team said, "We're nice people, John, and we're known as a nice church. And we don't want to lose that." She continued, "We still want to be nice!" I smiled and said, "It's nice to be nice, but maybe it's time you stopped being nice and started being Christlike. Maybe instead of being nice, you could be audaciously loving and see what happens. Maybe it's time we started incarnating the compassionate activist heart of Jesus." There were a couple of quiet "Amens" and a lot of silence. I knew I was asking a great deal from them. I knew it was a lot easier to make some trays of egg salad and be welcoming to people. There's certainly nothing wrong with those things (in fact, they're necessary, too) but there is more that we can and need to do as agents of divine love.

Jesus wasn't always nice. He was always love, but not a soft, saccharine, Hallmark-movie, pop song love. He flipped the tables of the temple vendors because of love for his Father's house. He ripped into the hypocritical religious leaders who leveraged their position and their power to exploit people—because of his love for those they manipulated. He declared that his mission was to be good news for the poor, the sick, the vulnerable, the imprisoned[6] because he loved them—which sounded like bad news to the wealthy and the powerful and the corrupt. As Mary declares with gratitude in Luke's Gospel, the work of God, which will continue through Jesus, "has brought down the powerful from their thrones, and lifted up the lowly; . . . filled the hungry with good things, and sent the rich away empty."[7] This is the inheritance we're here to steward both individually and collectively.

OVERVALUING NICENESS

SANITIZING JESUS' FIERCE LOVE FOR HUMANITY

A love that looks like Jesus is fierce and audacious and bold and courageous.

A love that looks like Jesus doesn't sit quietly while bigotry bullies the most vulnerable.

A love that looks like Jesus will not be tone policed into making nice with discrimination.

A love that looks like Jesus does not apologize for its passion for humanity.

A love that looks like Jesus will not wilt when it is labeled too political.

A love that looks like Jesus is dangerous to injustice, it confronts ugliness, it welcomes turbulence.

A love that looks like Jesus will drive us out of the safety of our privilege and into the discomfort of the trenches.

A love that looks like Jesus will be called political and angry and it will love anyway.

I am OK being labeled angry. I'm just going to keep making sure my anger is directed at the right person, to the right extent, at the right time, with the right motive, and in the right way.

Stay angry, good people.

Chapter 15
LOVE YOUR
DAMN NEIGHBOR

If you call your local cable provider to order service, at some point in the conversation, invariably the customer service representative will make you an offer: if you'd like to also add internet and phone service, they can package these services, and they will be much more affordable than if you purchased them separately or elsewhere. This is what is known as *bundling*. Life is supposedly better when you bundle. Life is easier when you bundle. I like bundling because it makes me feel like I'm getting something for free—and I've had lots of practice at that.

I recently turned fifty-one years old, and I'm more than a little embarrassed to say that it took far too many of those years to even begin to understand that as a white, cisgender, heterosexual man who identifies as Christian, I have the Privilege Bundle—and it was prepaid long before I arrived. I was grandfathered (or great-great-great-grandfathered) in, so to speak. The color of my skin, my gender, my sexual orientation, my profession of faith, my very physicality—all buffered me from many varieties of adversity, formed a barrier against a great deal of struggle others experience as routine, opened doors that I never realized had been opened, and afforded me a vast multitude of advantages—some of which I'll become aware of and others (despite all efforts) that I'll remain oblivious to. At the core of this learning is the realization that I have been the beneficiary of inequity.

But that wasn't the story I would have told you through the first few decades of my life. I lived with a set of assumptions based largely on the particular arrangement of my privilege. (You have one based on yours, as well.) Back then, I would have told you that anyone who wanted to work hard had the same opportunities to succeed, even though, if my mother were writing this, she'd tell you that I often didn't work very hard and still somehow managed to usually find success. This is one of the painful realities people of profound privilege need to reckon with: how much more effort those without it are required to expend in order to achieve similar opportunity, recognition, or reward. Earlier in my journey, I would have told you that everyone who desired one had equal access to an education—all while attending a private school many families couldn't afford, having two parents who were fully engaged in my life, and never wanting for a meal or clothes or transportation or well-paid teachers or conditions that allowed me to thrive. I would have told you that anyone who followed the rules, obeyed the law, and behaved respectfully would have nothing to fear during a traffic stop—yet I can remember being in the backseat of our car when my father was pulled over for speeding in a school zone, and before the officer even reached the window, my father yelled, "Just give me the effin' ticket!" (And miraculously, he just gave my father the effin' ticket.)

So, even though so much of my experiential evidence testified loudly in opposition to my working assumptions about the world, I held tightly to those fictional stories because I needed them to be accurate. I stayed committed to a narrative about the world I wanted to be true, because the alternative was to have my world turned upside down by the inequity around me. This is the seductive power of privilege: The more you benefit from a system, the easier it is to defend that system. The greater advantages the status quo provides you, the more tempted you'll be to resist changes in it. When you've always had the best and most comfortable seat at the table, it is really difficult to imagine that there are people waiting outside. When you are a beneficiary of inequity—equity often isn't a priority. When you are a beneficiary of inequity, you will naturally be oblivious to or shielded from injustices experienced by those inequity most endangers—and your religion will be affected similarly. You will have biases that get incorporated into your theology without you realizing it. When you are a beneficiary of inequity, equity may bring some discomfort with it. I want you to think about your specific and unprecedented bundle of privilege, because that has shaped your story and because that story can be your greatest teacher if it gets a little help.

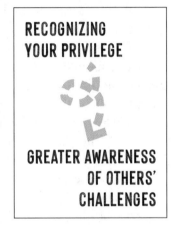

RECOGNIZING
YOUR PRIVILEGE

GREATER AWARENESS
OF OTHERS'
CHALLENGES

Our stories all have a specific geography, a precise place and time where we find ourselves—a "local neighborhood" where we have our assumptions built, our prejudices formed, and our blind spots created. It's also where we build relationships and impact lives and engage the brokenness. For the past twenty-five years, my "neighborhood" has been the Church, specifically predominately white churches in the South, as a pastor. My first church was diverse. For proof, all you had to do was visit our website. It said we were diverse. In reality, our church's racial diversity spanned from white to beige—and everything in between. As a white, cisgender, heterosexual male pastor of a largely white church, I felt a growing tension as I began to understand that few entities in America have been more powerful agents of inequity than the Christian Church—along lines of race and gender and sexual orientation and socioeconomic level. If Jesus was the builder of the bigger table, organized Christianity has often taken a chainsaw to it. That isn't really up for debate. The only present question is whether or not we can still put it back together, and the answer's going to come down to how willing we are to get the better stories and to get a closer view of people we've lost the ability to see clearly from where we've been standing.

At their best, all our "neighborhoods" (including our churches) naturally breed a sense of affinity and intimacy, which is a beautiful thing—but if we're not careful we can gradually grow insular, leery of people outside of it, protective of whoever we imagine "our own" to be. When that happens, it can become easy to see only the commonalities of people close to us and what appear to be vast differences between us and those we only see from a distance. In both religion and politics, this often breeds a subtle bias against perceived outsiders and gives us a lower tolerance for disagreement with them. We believe the best of our tribe and think the worst of everyone else. This certainly happens from time to time in even the most open faith communities, and we've all likely been on both the giving and receiving ends of this exclusion.

We tend to complicate life and religion, but sometimes the obvious answer *is* the answer. Sometimes you just need to get closer to people to see them more clearly, proximity usually being the best teacher. That can be difficult to remember in days when our most common interactions with people are through the buffer of social media tribalism, where we can easily reduce them to stereotypes, caricatures, and perfectly crafted enemy avatars or partisan meme fodder. Religion at its best should be a gravitational force that pulls human beings toward one another as we consider the divinity reflected in the humanity of other. It should remove the distance between people, not magnify it, and people who take the greatest commandment seriously do the hard work of inviting and moving toward.

Not long after the 2016 presidential election in America, my dear friend Susan noticed how fractured and contentious the country had become, how genuine dialogue had begun to break down, and she grieved it fully. Instead of allowing the enormity of the discord to freeze her, she decided to do something as elemental as it was redemptive: she decided to get closer to her enemies. Susan had grown up in the Southern Baptist Church and currently identifies as a Unitarian Universalist (which represents a fairly long spiritual journey). Through her friendships and social media connections, she began inviting women into her home every Sunday to have lunch and play bridge. Rather than use the occasion to settle into a secure weekly bunker of like-minded, agreeable progressive cohorts, she intentionally filled her home with women whose theological and political views were diametrically opposite her own. (Think Franklin Graham devotionals and MAGA hats.) These were other middle-aged white women, also raised in the South and weaned on sweet tea, fresh biscuits, and bless-your-heart Bible Belt evangelicalism. Susan's motive wasn't to change or fix or convert her guests (though she confessed a slight move away from the Dark Side would be a welcomed Bob Ross "happy accident"), it was to hear their stories, build a genuine relationship, and learn about these women what she couldn't learn from a distance or in the safety of an echo chamber. This sacred proximity characterized the Jesus she grew up reading about in Sunday school, who dined with the religious leaders, tax collectors, and street rabble, so she figured it could work for her too: a very different kind of Sunday school.

At this point, you might be tempted to imagine Susan's home as some sweetly soundtracked Christmas Day Ebenezer Scrooge scene of genuine repentance and full transformation.[1] Don't. These gatherings were often a disaster. In many conversations on Sunday mornings, she'd look at me, exasperated, and say, "Have you seen the news this week? If you still pray, pray for me because we're going to have to deal with all *that* later today!" The process has been grueling and uncomfortable at times, but there have been moments of brilliant light breaking in. A couple months ago, Susan shared a revelatory moment around her dining room table. The conversation drifted into the Black Lives Matter movement and the gaping racial divide in the country. As the women did their best to delicately navigate the potential minefield laid out in front of them over mounds of homemade fried chicken, one of them began to look wistfully off in the distance, and tears clouded her eyes. Susan asked, "Why are you crying?" to which the woman said after a thoughtful pause: "I just don't know why God made other races." (At this point I was grateful that I hadn't been present. I'd have probably responded by reminding the woman that if Adam and Eve had existed, they definitely weren't Caucasian—or that the cradle of civilization didn't come with a Cracker

Barrel.) Thankfully, Susan is wiser and less impulsive than I am. "Tell me more," she said. "Well," her clearly shaken tablemate replied, "if God hadn't made other races then there wouldn't be racism and we'd all get along."

Susan's encounter reminds us how powerful our origin stories are, how they shape the way we see the world and imagine God and craft our biases. The woman across from her was genuinely grieving the fractures she could see from where she was; she was deeply troubled at the visible divisions—but she was viewing them through lenses that distorted the *whys* of their existence. She wasn't a bad person; she was a good person with a bad story. Either because of the theology she was raised in or the childhood lessons handed down by the adults in her life or the media she's been exposed to, her working mythology of the world told her that *her whiteness* was the norm, the base-setting pigmentation of humanity—and that anything outside of that constituted "other races," and was somehow less-than. With this working assumption, it's perfectly reasonable to understand why she'd assume that God is white. For this woman, these conclusions aren't racist impulses or intentional supremacist declarations, they're a natural takeaway based on the information she's been given. She has a bad Christian story, the kind many have been weaned on. The God of this story is volatile, capricious, and decidedly unloving, and that puts distance between them and so many

BEING EXPOSED TO DIFFERENT STORIES

EXPANDING OUR UNDERSTANDING OF GOD AND THE WORLD

people in their path. We all know people like Susan's lunch guest: really good people with some really bad God stories. These stories make racism, homophobia, nationalism, and misogyny logical by-products.

Many of us came out of a Christianity with a bad story, or we bear the scars of bad-story Christians with a tragically undersized God. In many ways, white evangelicalism is built largely on an inequitable theology: the fraudulent premise that God is a cisgender, heterosexual white guy who was born in America, identifies as Christian, and was raised Republican. With that as its operating system, it is going to intentionally or subconsciously perpetuate injustice against people who don't fit that very narrow list of qualifiers—and it will cause the churches these people fill or oversee to resist changes that bring any movement toward balance in a world that for thousands of years has been decidedly tipped in their favor. This default religious worldview renders people unable to see clearly, because doing so would challenge and possibly completely upend their entire God story. This is why Susan's investment in those draining, bombastic Sunday afternoons is both costly and priceless. Without her steadfast presence and her genuine desire to learn why someone believes differently than she does, she wouldn't be at that table when a fifty-five-year-old woman afflicted with privilege begins to recognize her symptoms, when she is vulnerable enough to name her grief and to let down her battle posture long enough to really listen, because she trusts the person across from her to see her as more than a stereotype. I think that's the messy, precarious spot where we can really love our neighbor even if we don't particularly like them—or like them but despise something they believe in. We begin with a posture of curiosity and we commit to learning something about them that we don't yet know.

The implications of a Maker who made *everything that has been made* are fairly knee-weakening when you consider the company you regularly keep. When you meet another person (whoever that person is) you are coming face-to-face with a once-in-history, never-to-be-repeated reflection of the image of God. This is true of the next person you meet and the hundreds you pass in traffic (even the guy you just flipped off), navigate around at the grocery store, and spar with on social media. If God is God, there's no other option: they are each made of God stuff, no matter how bitter, cruel, or petty they might be or how unlikable you find them or how difficult to like they indeed might be. Every single day you encounter thousands of breathing, animated thumbnails of the Divine. None of them capture it in totality, but every person is a small piece. In this way, we might begin to understand God as the sum total of eight billion extraordinary fragments stitched together. I suppose that if God is love and if love is universal, then a universal God is the only accurate understanding. It would be the height of arrogance to say to a Muslim or a Jew or a Buddhist or a Sikh or to anyone of any authentic, sincere perspective, "Your story may be meaningful and life-giving to you, but it's wrong." How small am I making God when I do that? How open am I to being led to a deeper and wider place? How big of a jerk does that make me?

Loving beyond our capabilities is almost always going to be inconvenient beforehand and beautiful afterward, rarely the other way around. Redemptive acts are often preceded by the fractures that necessitate them. (Something needs repair because it is broken: a relationship, a system, a nation.) No matter what story we tell ourselves when we put people on blast or shout them down or block them on social media, nothing feels as good as when we show someone more decency than they may deserve, when we err on the side of loving them—even if their response is less than appreciative.

The way you treat other people is the only meaningful expression of your belief system anyway; it is the space where your values are on full display. Theologians and seminary students call this *orthopraxy* (your actions) as opposed to *orthodoxy* (your beliefs). Jesus called it the "fruit"[2] of a life: the tangible, visible, feel-able part of human beings that reflects whatever has taken root in their hearts. Most people call it being a person of your word. When it comes to the heart of it all, your religion isn't what you believe, your religion is how you treat people. The only real theology that's of worth is relational theology. It exists in no other way that is meaningful to another human being. Whatever you have floating around inside your head or might preach about regarding a God of love is ultimately inconsequential. Your beliefs take the infinite, stratospheric, wonder-filled things of the cosmos and shrink them down into something you can hold in your hand. As we live alongside people, the theoretical and the abstract become tangible, personal realities. Our theological stance is revealed in the small places where our lives rub shoulders with someone else's. It's really easy to parrot back that you "love your neighbor" but a far greater challenge to love your actual neighbor when your neighbor is an abject jackass.

Our convictions and doctrines and moral codes only exist to the extent that we are willing and able to incarnate them. Jesus sets the table he does because his heart compels him to. Once in a while, we act our way into belief, or we do something that leads us to a revelation or alters our world-view. More often though, our moral center propels us into the world, orients us, directs our eyes, animates our beings. If you want to know what you really believe, play back this day in reverse in your head, and that will tell you—it certainly told the people you interacted with. In other words, if you're a person of faith, you can't have a bigger table with a tiny God.

Our undersized theology is usually revealed by those we seek to exclude, the people who draw our animosity. Our tendency toward exclusion is an alarm telling us we have growing to do. For as vociferously as white evangelicals in America profess to be reborn through and compelled by the boundless grace of God, practically speaking their religion is frequently defined by those it vilifies, condemns, and excludes—which turns out to be an extensive list. It claims to offer unmerited grace but requires that it be asked for and earned. It has devolved into damnation from a distance.

We human beings tend to be emotionally lazy. We're prone to taking the feelings of least resistance. As we move through the day and as people cross our paths, we usually settle for whatever thoughts come immediately, the ones that don't take much work: the knee-jerk responses they trigger in us upon contact, whether this is affection or contempt. As a result, we usually don't spend much time concerning ourselves with those who disagree with us— their complexity, their backstories, their internal condition. This is perhaps most true of our politics and our religious beliefs, which—like it or not—are conjoined twins. They are not distinct, separated compartments, they are one and the same: personal morality is internal, and our politics make that morality tactile—and these things are at the mercy of the unnatural tempo of our lives. At the artificially accelerated pace at which we live and move through the world, we simply don't have time to linger with people long enough to really see them or hear them, to go beyond a cursory diagnosis of them, let alone imagine they might have a perspective we could learn from—or worse yet, that we might actually like them despite not wanting to. We grab a quick cue from their social media profiles, churches, T-shirts, and bumper stickers—a political cue, a religious expression, a retweet source—and on that spindly and fragile skeleton, we instantly construct a living avatar to which we can attach all our fears, biases, and past wounds.

Toxic tribalism thrives in such relational shorthand: we can view someone across the social media chasm, and in an instant size them up, remove any nuance or humanity, and fully caricature them into the irredeemable adversary we need. That makes hating them much easier for us—and hating them is just a hell of a lot quicker and simpler than knowing or understanding them. Not only do we get to be jerks—but self-righteous ones at that.

People ask me all the time, "How do we move forward when there is so much bitterness and discord in the world?" They usually don't like the answer—although I often don't like it much either. It starts in the mirror, and that's the last place we look for hypocrites and frauds.

During the 2018 midterm elections, I spent a week with Vote Common Good, a traveling caravan of progressive speakers, ministers, and musicians, canvassing the nation in a former Guns N' Roses tour bus and telling conservative white evangelicals that not only could they vote along a different party line while affirming their spiritual convictions—but that in this unprecedented climate, they should.

Our closing night rally was to be in the parking lot of a Fresno, California, church. A couple of days before we arrived, rumors began circulating that we'd be visited by the Proud Boys, a group of alt-right activists known for physical intimidation and for inciting violence at progressive political and religious

RECOGNIZING THE INTERCONNECTEDNESS OF RELIGION AND POLITICS

CLEARER ASSESSMENT OF OUR MOTIVATIONS

events and claiming self-defense while responding tenfold. We'd been warned several times before in different cities along the tour that the group might be showing up, but they'd always failed to materialize, so as night fell it seemed the same would hold true.

As I stood to the side of our portable stage taking in the scene, out of the corner of my eye I noticed a small cluster of people, illuminated by video cameras and phones, emerging from the darkened periphery of the parking lot and walking until they reached the last row of chairs assembled on the blacktop. The group began quietly at first, then steadily grew louder, laughing sarcastically and yelling over our speakers while waving signs and livestreaming the event to their followers and fans watching in real time. I could feel my blood pressure rising and my face getting hot as I prepared to speak. I milled around the uninvited instigators and grew more and more concerned for my friend Kristy, who was trying

to politely speak over their more frequent and fervent interruption. When she finished and descended the short metal
staircase, I made my way up and took the platform, already
fully enraged, adrenaline coursing wildly through me like
a mid-Hulkout Bruce Banner—and since I'd decided that
velocity and volume were my best defenses, I grabbed the
microphone tightly and proceeded to shout loudly and without pausing for more than a fraction of a second (lest I give
the protesters a space to be heard). Like a sweaty, deranged,
pissed-off auctioneer, I breathlessly fired off rapid, raw-
throated verbal grenades about the gentle and expansive love
of a peacemaking Jesus—which I'd screamed until my throat
was raw, while simultaneously hoping for God to send a swift
wind to evict them from the county. The irony was not lost on
me. When I finished my final staccato salvo, I hurried off the
stage and stood behind the parked tour bus, feeling like I'd
succeeded only in being louder and ruder than they were—
and that didn't feel like much of a victory.

My dear friend Genesis Be took the platform immediately following me. Gen is a brilliant musician, poet, activist, a woman of color, and probably twenty years younger
than me. I felt protective of her in that moment and stepped
out from behind the bus, waiting for what I was sure was
going to be a moment necessitating physical intervention.
As she began to softly speak about growing up in Missis-
sippi as a biracial person in a home that was both Christian
and Muslim, the Proud Boys began to heckle her as they'd
done to me and the previous speakers—but she responded
differently.

"Before I share my story," she said, turning and looking directly at them, "I want to speak to my potential future
co-collaborators back there." Still looking directly at them,
she said, "I don't see you as my enemies, but my potential

co-collaborators." It seemed as if someone pressed a mute button on the rest of the world, because the only thing I could hear was her voice and the quiet hum of the PA between her words.

She smiled warmly and went further. "I want to know if any of you back there would be willing to come up here and embrace me."

After a few still and silent seconds, one of the men began walking from the back row, still recording on his phone. He jumped up onto the center of the platform, and Genesis opened her arms widely and hugged him tightly and told him she loved him, and he responded in kind. She whispered, "I don't agree with you, but I love you." Applause erupted from the platform and the audience and even from the protesters. The man soon returned to his place at the back of the crowd and continued to talk back the rest of the night, but never as loudly or angrily as he had. His rage had been disarmed by its radical counterpoint. I don't know if Genesis's actions changed him—but they changed many of us. They changed me.

Later, as our team sat at the edge of the parking lot and reflected on the evening, more than a few of us relayed the fear we felt, especially for Genesis. She said matter-of-factly and with great empathy: "I've met people like this my whole life, and so I wasn't scared. I know they're frightened."

Genesis had far more reason not to let these people off the hook than a cisgender, heterosexual, white guy afflicted with privilege like myself, much more right to return venom for venom and insult for insult, far more cause to put them fully on blast there with the lights and the microphone—but she didn't. She saw their humanity, showed them her own, and left it in their hands whether they were going to honor that humanity or not. She incarnated the very biggest love in the face of a clear lack of love—because the scale of the God she aspires to compels her to. Jesus said if we love only those who love us, we don't really get credit for that.[3] That's baseline human stuff. Honors-level spirituality loves those who seem most unlovable, subject us to the greatest hatred, and require the greatest courage.

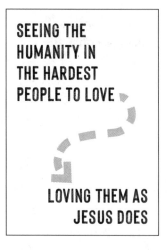

SEEING THE HUMANITY IN THE HARDEST PEOPLE TO LOVE

LOVING THEM AS JESUS DOES

I'm not asking you to embrace a violent white supremacist or to place yourself in the path of physical harm or to do anything that causes you emotional injury. But generally speaking, if our faith is going to overcome the ugliness around us, we're all going to have to figure out how to do the difficult work of loving people we dislike. We're going to have to stop creating false stories about people from a safe distance and get truer stories. We're going to have to find a way to offer an open hand instead of a clenched fist. We're going to need to slow down enough and get close enough to our supposed enemies that we can look in the whites of their eyes and find the goodness residing behind them. It may be buried in jagged layers of fear and grief and hopelessness—but it is almost always there. I don't like to think about the humanity of people when they are acting inhumanely and find ironically that I have the greatest difficulty manufacturing compassion for people who seem to lack compassion, mostly because I don't want them to get away with something. I don't want to risk giving tacit consent to the terrible things they do, to the wounds they inflict, to the violence they manufacture—and the simplest way to do this seems to be to despise them. Hating people is always going to be the easier and more expedient path than loving them, because loving them means seeing them fully, hearing their story, stepping into their skin and shoes as best we can, and finding something worth embracing. I wonder if we can do that. I wonder if I can. That's a pretty worthwhile prayer.

Chapter 16
THE CHURCH OF
NOT BEING HORRIBLE

One of my favorite scenes from Christopher Guest's brilliant mock rock documentary *This Is Spinal Tap* shows the struggling and aging band's beleaguered manager Ian Faith sitting in a hotel room, excitedly critiquing what he believes to be an artist's scale model of his client's planned massive stage reproduction of Stonehenge, meant to bring the band back to their theatrical rock-show glory days.[1] His follow-up questions to the sculptor about how the "real thing" will look in comparison to the piece yield confusion at first, and ultimately the horrifying revelation: this *is* the real thing. Due to an incorrect notation scribbled on a napkin in a fit of inspiration by guitarist Nigel Tufnel, the artist had been mistakenly instructed to construct a piece eighteen *inches,* not eighteen feet, tall. The scene immediately cuts to the oblivious band on stage in front of a rapt audience, in all their earnest self-seriousness, as they reach the climactic moment of the song. We witness their abject confusion as the woefully undersized monument descends from the rafters and two little people in medieval garb dance around it to the sounds of lute playing while towering mightily over the structure (to humorous and decidedly *not* awe-inspiring effect). This seems to be what far too many of the churches in America have become in the eyes of people looking in from the outside: a misguided production that has reduced something massive and mysterious to a laughable fraction of itself, because somewhere along the way something important got lost in translation.

"We have to win people for Christ."

Over the past few decades, I've heard this phrase come out of the mouths of Christians somewhere in the neighborhood of eight billion times (though I'll admit my calculations may be off slightly). The point is, I've heard it *a lot*—from pastors, evangelists, worship leaders, small-group members, young missionaries, and Christian neighbors—and I've rarely felt comfortable when I have. It's always sounded like a stray sour note in a jazz guitarist's run that wasn't in the right key: a jarring dissonance. There's something about the evangelical war language of conquest and victory and about people as spiritual commodities in soul transactions that feels sharply incongruous with the community defined by love that Jesus curated while here.

The *pre-Christianity* Christianity that was meant to serve as the blueprint was an organic movement of the street; a mysterious, elevating, yeast-in-the-dough[2] reaction triggered by the unlikely gathering of the rejected and the marginalized and the poor. Before it ever had a name, the Church was this motley assortment of fishermen, farmers, prostitutes, and tax collectors all led in example by a homeless, itinerant preacher as they found affinity in his countercultural invitation to love radically and to live interdependently. Without buildings or lobbyists or national boycotts or culture wars, it was exactly what it was initially designed to be: an imperfect, interdependent community that protected its most vulnerable. It was the *visibly different* people who tangibly altered the places they traveled in life-giving ways. Birthed in the heart of the Roman Empire, with all its might, greed, and coercive power, Christianity was the humble, compassionate, generous resistance to all of it—and this is the problem we have right now in America if we profess Christianity.

Somewhere during the past two thousand years we've flipped the script of our collective spiritual story, and in many ways we are now an inverted people—an upside-down community to the world and likely at times to Jesus. This *burdened-to-win* religion currently trying to eat up market share and mandate compliance here is Rome. It is the *hypocritical religious elite*. It is the *wide road* that Jesus said leads to destruction. It is the *love of money* at the root of evil. It is the very thing Jesus rejected with every fiber of his being—and if we're to resurrect the heart

A PREOCCUPATION WITH SAVING SOULS

THE TEMPTATION TO IGNORE PRESENT SUFFERING

of Jesus in this place and time, this toxic religion needs to die. Christianity as modeled by Jesus was never meant to hold power. It was never supposed to be dominant. It was never about control or brute force or dictating the laws of the land or imposing itself on people's lives. It was certainly never about cozying up to national leaders with no regard for humanity. Someone needs to remind the Church and the Republican Party of that. Someone needs to preach it to the Bible Belt, and to the celebrity pastors, and to the Christians who don't realize just how much they've lost the plot and just how they've become the opposition to the author and perfecter of their declared faith. Someone needs to inconvenience these comfortable Christians with the actual words of Jesus. World domination wasn't the plan. World renovation was.

I've always joked that I was going to start a new church: The Church of Not Being Horrible. Our mission statement would simply be *Don't be horrible to people.* Our *what we believe* doctrinal statements would be replaced by *how we treat people* promises: Don't treat them as less worthy of love, respect, dignity, joy, and opportunity than you are. Don't create caricatures of them based on their skin color, their religion, their sexual orientation, the amount of money they have, or the circumstances they find themselves in. Don't seek to take away things from them that you already enjoy in abundance: civil rights, clean water, education, marriage, access to health care. Don't tell someone's story for them about why they are poor, depressed, addicted, victimized, or alone. Let them tell their story and believe they know it better than you do. Don't imagine that your experience of the world is everyone's experience of the world; that the ease, comfort, support, affection you have received are universal. Don't be preoccupied with how someone experiences God, how they define family, whom they love. Cultivate *your own* faith, family, and marriage.

The central question at any given moment in the Church of Not Being Horrible is, *Am I being horrible right now?* If one concludes that they *are,* they endeavor to not do so. They lean into authentic relationships and they allow other people to help them see their blind spots of privilege, prejudice, and ignorance (the stuff that tends to make us horrible) and then they respond with an activated life that moves with a new intention. In other words, our sacred calling is to be decent, to be kind, to be compassionate, to be whatever it is that we believe this place is lacking: to be the kind of people the world needs—and it definitely needs less horrible these days.

The Church of Not Being Horrible would gather every week to celebrate the inherent goodness of people; to share stories of the ways we succeeded in being less horrible to our families, coworkers, and strangers; and to challenge ourselves to be even less horrible in the coming week. We'd do this faithfully, repeatedly, and passionately, and hopefully we'd begin to watch the world around us gradually become less angry, less bitter, and less painful. It may seem like a low bar to set, but it's actually a beautiful aspiration. Again, you don't need a church in order to not be horrible—but if you *are* a community of faith in whatever way you measure such things, horrible had better not be your calling card, or you're doing something really wrong. To the poor and the oppressed and the marginalized around you, you should be really good news. Many Christian communities have managed to flip the inclusive, generous, expansive script Jesus began with—but there are millions of people really trying to get it right. They're reminding us that God was always been in the business of beautiful surprises.

The Old Testament tells the superhero origin story of Moses, the Hebrew and Christian traditions' soon-to-be patriarch, who is tending to the flocks in desolate wilderness when he is greeted by an angel who famously inhabits a burning bush and instructs him to take off his sandals because his feet are on holy ground. In this freshly anointed sacred space, the story says, God relates his desire to emancipate the Israelites from Pharaoh's death grip using an unheralded, inexperienced Moses to this unfathomable end. For me, the revelatory part of the passage isn't a supernatural figure showing up in some singed shrubbery to deliver a Rocky Balboa–style motivational speech to a dark-horse would-be hero of three faith traditions—it's the idea that divinity transcends expectation, that the presence of God is limitless, not only in its forms but in its geography; that all ground is potentially holy if your eyes are open and your heart is pliable. If you operate from a place of love, every person is sacred and every place is sanctified and each moment is bless-able.

The moment I stepped on Beit T'Shuvah's West Los Angeles campus, a sprawling collection of oddly connected brick buildings, I felt I needed to quickly remove my shoes.[3] I'd been invited there by the organization's founder and leader, Rabbi Mark Borovitz:

FORGETTING ABOUT POWER AND POLISH

A MORE CHRISTLIKE MOVEMENT

an irascible, irreverent, fiercely loving, fedora-wearing Jewish preacher whose road had traveled through addiction and prison before delivering him here as the architect of what the organization's website describes as "a residential addiction treatment center, congregation, and educational institute where life is celebrated and every soul matters." Weeks earlier, in preparation for the messages I'd soon be delivering there, I'd wondered if I'd be speaking to a progressive Jewish faith community, to a secular gathering of human beings in recovery, or to a nondenominational collection of flawed people exploring their inherent worth. If there'd been any bushes nearby as I pondered this, I might have received the simple answer "Yes." The delineations of my questions were small God concerns. In a matter of minutes on site, I realized that I'd be sharing sacred space with beautifully strange humans in the thinnest of places.

In 2016, I wrote a book called *A Bigger Table*, dreaming about a place where disparate people could gather in redemptive spiritual community that allowed them each to be received without caveat or condition. Standing in Beit T'Shuvah, I felt as if I'd stepped into the tangible embodiment of those aspirational words. I'd call Rabbi Borovitz's working theology "belovedness," and as elemental as that seems, it's revolutionary to experience. There are weekly Friday night and Saturday services heavily steeped in Jewish tradition and ritual, along with a wealth of unorthodox and surprising additions: 12-step language, an exuberant blues-based house band, references to the teaching of Jesus, occasional cussing, and frequent off-script interruptions by people moved to offer a testimony or word of encouragement or to preach whatever sermon had formed within them. Rabbi Mark and his wife, longtime social worker and author Harriet Borovitz, held their initial plans and restrictions on the center loosely, allowing the community to become what they couldn't conceive of at the time, which is often the best way to invite something God-sized: getting your own will out of the way and making a plan that you expect to revise. They were compelled simply to make hurting people feel loved and to let them respond accordingly.

Lately, I find that all loving spiritual communities are recovery communities in some form or another. They are spaces to acknowledge failures and admit flaws, to work through issues and overcome obstacles, and sometimes to grieve the sustained losses and necessary separations that come with growth. They are places that allow you to fall and give you a way to get back up because they understand how easy falling is. So many spiritual communities begin with a carefully calculated vision, with everything from the graphics to the services to the ministries tightly focus-grouped into a safe sterility that weeds out anything messy or uncomfortable or unwieldy. The problem is, messy and uncomfortable and unwieldy are usually where the unboxed glory and expansive love we really need shows up: outside the lines, beyond the boundaries, in the surprises, within the failures. The myth of local churches is that their health is determined by their lack of conflict and the absence of turbulence, but just as with enduring marriages and life-long friendships (or my big, loud Italian family), sometimes relational honesty generates bombastic exchanges, creates unpleasant conversations, and yields genuine discomfort, and these things aren't necessarily signs of sickness, but proof of life.

The most transformative communities are places where people live together in the unknowing, admitting that they're trying to figure out the *un-figure-out-able*, and giving each other a break when they understandably fall on their faces. Honest religious communities are messy, unwieldy places populated by well-meaning underachiev-ers, disappointed dreamers, and exposed impostors. That's all they've ever been. Christians often sanitize the early Church in the book of Acts as some fuzzy, *kumbaya* com-mune of free love and hippie Jesus good vibes—but the Bible tells us there were ego clashes and despicable betray-als and public shade-throwing and hostile ministry take-overs—which sounds a lot closer to what we experience and are frustrated by in our own faith communities. Maybe if we start by admitting that, we can save ourselves from the unre-alistic expectations about spiritual community that they

weren't designed for or capable of—and just revel in the
disorienting relational messiness of authentic life together.

A few months before the COVID crisis began (back before
we regularly used terms like "social distancing," "self-
isolation," and "flattening the curve"), I was leading a weekend mountain retreat near North Carolina's stunning Blue
Ridge Mountains. As I waited for guests to arrive for orientation on the first night, my emotions pinballed erratically
back and forth between soaring expectancy and abject terror. Like all party or event hosts, I held both the potential
jubilation of what might be coming if things worked out
well—and the heavy dread that no one would show up and
I'd end up sitting there alone like a jilted prom date. My
fears proved unfounded, as first gradually and then rapidly
the large room began to fill, crackling with the buzz of new
stories intersecting and the beautiful noise of warm intro-
ductions. Suddenly, a woman with dark-rimmed glasses and
salt-and-pepper hair piled in a loose bun on top of her head
exploded through the door like a fierce gust of wind, pulling the attention of the room to her and creating an instant
silence. She looked around at the assembled humanity and
exhaled deeply, extended her arms, tilted her head back,
and shouted, "MY PEOPLE!" I quickly replied in as dead-
pan a fashion as I could: "I'm sorry, ma'am, you're in the
wrong room—*your* people are actually meeting down the
hall." The room erupted into laughter and robust embraces
all around. Most of the people in that room were complete
strangers a few moments earlier, yet because they had a
point of commonality (which, in this case, just happened
to be my writing), they knew enough about the gathering
and those who'd be showing up to be sure they would be

welcomed in their present condition: that there were certain givens in place ensuring their acceptance, hoops they weren't going to be required to jump through, moral litmus tests they wouldn't need to pass. They knew that while they may often feel the slow suffocation of being loved with caveats and conditions or tolerated with coldness or rejected outright—in this room they would be able to stop and breathe again. I think God's presence does this. I think love makes you feel like you can exhale.

At a fall tour stop in Austin, a young Latino couple named Luis and Maria came up and introduced themselves shortly before my talk. They told me they'd driven nearly ten hours from New Mexico to be there, explaining that living surrounded by a conservative family in a very small, conservative town, they felt alone and isolated most of the time, unable to share their religious and political convictions fully for fear of rejection and even expulsion. As Maria wiped a tear away, Luis said, "We just wanted to be in a room with people who get us." I knew exactly what he meant. It's exhausting to feel you have to constantly try to conceal the truest parts of yourself from people you're supposed to be most open with; to couch your language and soften your opinions and maintain a carefully constructed facade in order keep a tenuous peace. Luis and Maria drove nearly half a day, entered a church they'd never been to, filled with people they'd never met before—just to feel *home.* As much as I was grateful they'd been able to do that, I grieved the fact that we'd be going our separate ways in a few hours, and that they would go back to feeling like orphans in their family, lepers in their church, and outsiders in their community—and that so many professed Christians would be responsible for making them feel that way.

There is something transformative and sacred in belonging. When we are received as we are, we can drop our defenses, breathe deeply, and trust that we don't need to earn or deserve a place; that unlike so many other places we find ourselves, there are no prerequisites or qualifiers hindering us there, no hidden agendas waiting to ensnare us, no eventual bait-and-switch coming. If there's anything spiritual community should do, it's this. It should give people a sense of found-ness. People experienced this in Jesus' presence, whether priest or prostitute, whether revered soldier or shamed pariah, whether confidently pious or morally bankrupt.

DIVERSE, OPEN SPIRITUAL COMMUNITY

A SENSE OF BELONGING AND BEING FOUND

This isn't what his Church is most known for lately, and that's a problem. Each year, I speak with thousands of people in my travels who've felt purposefully discarded by Christians and by the churches they frequent: forced prodigals who are pushed to the periphery and never allowed to feel fully welcomed in their midst because of their gender identity, sexual orientation, nation of origin, theological beliefs, or past experience. Most of us know what it is like to be denied proximity or accepted with provisions. Communities that profess to be oriented toward God should be spaces where disparate human beings should find safety upon arrival. They should be marked by the emancipation from striving; they should be such breathing places. This kind of belonging is what the world is starved for and what spiritual people can give it. While disconnection and exclusion characterize so much of the landscape of our days, we can make spaces for the exhale of simply being home. That expansive welcome and intimate kindness are the holy ground that the best of religion prepares for people to rest upon.

D uring a Q&A following a session at Wild Goose Festival, a man asked if I ever considered starting a church. I answered that I didn't think so, because many situations would require me to be less than fully authentic, and I value being able to speak freely on the issues that matter to me without being beholden to a restrictive system. That freedom has allowed me to communicate with specificity and clarity where I might not otherwise have been able to. Later he came up and identified himself as an atheist. He said, "I think you should reconsider." The man shared with me that he and other atheist friends have been following my blog; it resonates with them, and he believes many people not currently at home in organized religion would be interested in being involved in something living out the values he sees in the writing. It gave me great pause. This has become a refrain I've heard echoed thousands of times over the past three years: people are hungry for redemptive community that makes the world more loving, more compassionate, and more decent—no matter what it's called. It reminded me that Jesus spent much of his life with both conservatively and liberally religious people, a great deal of it with nonreligious people—and *all* of it with non-Christians. He set in motion a revolution of radical hospitality and counterintuitive love that defied precedent and confounded those who imagined themselves righteous. Maybe my atheist friend is on to something.

There's a moment in the Gospel of Matthew where Jesus says to the religious leaders who believed they had the market cornered on God, "The tax collectors and the prostitutes are going into the kingdom of God ahead of you."[4] In other words, Jesus is saying, "These people, the ones you judge and condemn and look down on—*they're* getting it. *They* have my heart. *You're* the lost ones!" He was warning the self-righteous that their punitive religion and its toxic arrogance had become a millstone around their necks, and that what he was building would be built without them unless they could be internally altered to the point that humility made them more welcoming. Little has changed in two thousand years. Now, just as then, many of the religious people commandeering the name of God have become the very thing Jesus warned the world against. They've become infected with hypocrisy, greed, and contempt—and they are preventing people from seeing anything resembling the abundant life he preached about. Just as when his feet were on the planet, Jesus is telling us that God has outgrown the box we've tried to build for God, and we'd better be open to a new thing because this old thing is no longer life-giving.

And yet, as part of me mourns what my faith tradition has become in these days, I'm also filled with a near-explosive sense of hope as I watch what is being born in response to it. I see a strangely beautiful congregation assembling: many of those who claim the Christian faith, alongside those who no longer feel at home in the Church, people of differing traditions, those who aren't sure what they believe, and those with no religious affiliation at all. I call them the Community of the Convinced. They know that diversity is the better path. They know interdependence is the point. They are *all* speaking together with a singular, steady, strong voice—one that declares the inherent value of all people, a love that knows no qualifiers, and the desire to live these days together well. It's as close to the thing Jesus was doing as anything I've seen before. The skeptics, backsliders, doubters, heretics, apostates, and "sinners" are building the redemptive community the world needs. It was the plan all along. People of every hue; men and women; straight, gay, bisexual, and transgender; the religious, agnostics, and atheists—they're all feeling the same pull toward goodness.

I'm not sure the Church of Not Being Horrible will catch on, as being horrible seems to be trending these days among religious people, but I think it's worth a shot. I think it might alter the homes, marriages, and communities we're living in, if not the very planet we're standing on. It might renovate the very hearts within our chests, themselves so prone to being horrible. It might help us become the best versions of ourselves. More and more I am certain that the Church that will be, the Church that needs to be (just as in the days of Jesus), will be redefined and renovated by those that organized religion disregards, ignores, and vilifies. It will be composed of the motley assortment of failures, frauds, and messes who realize that the table isn't big enough yet— but that it's worth building, no matter what it's called. Jesus was a carpenter. He knows about building things.

Chapter 17
HIGH HORSES AND BETTER ANGELS

We recently welcomed a new addition to our family: Charlie, a twelve-week-old hound-mix rescue who arrived the night before pandemic lockdowns began here in North Carolina. The shelter was closing the next day and needed to place as many dogs in new homes as possible. The urgency of the moment pushed our family from curious browsers to instant adopters, and we soon headed to the pet store for emergency supplies, with a tiny black and tan ball of fur ping-ponging from window to window. Charlie immediately doubled our dog population, joining our eight-year-old Shepherd mix, Zoe, who quickly proved to be a surprisingly hospitable older sister. After an awkward hour of barking, bowing, hindquarter-sniffing canine conversation between the two of them (I assumed about Zoe's house rules and her expectations for the new kid), they bonded quickly.

A few days after Charlie's arrival I sat on the living room rug, strewn with half-chewed rawhide rolls and frayed pull toys, and gave the pups some quality time. Soon after, my wife walked in, looked at the floor around her, and said, "Well, someone's tracked something in!" I stood up to investigate; to my horror, I noticed dozens of brown streaks dotting the rug and surrounding hardwoods. "Is that . . . ?" she asked. I knew what she meant. She meant *not mud*. Worse, my sudden and violent gag reflex told me that, indeed, it was *not mud*. As I suppressed the growing urge to vomit, I sprang into action, seeking out which of my hairy housemates had brought this stinking pox upon our house. I noticed more and larger smears where I'd just been sitting and now around where I was standing. It was as if the stains were somehow rapidly multiplying! I leaned against the couch and tipped my foot over, and the truth suddenly hit me like an atomic stink bomb: I'd been the carrier. I was the one who'd stepped in it. This mess was 100 percent mine. I apologized to the dogs and my wife, in that order. Then, I threw up.

Moral superiority is a nice delusion if you can manage it: believing your particular mess is somehow superior to someone else's, or pinpointing them as the cause of everything ailing humanity. It is often conservative religion's primary engine upon which the whole thing runs: identify an enemy and go to war, certain you're defending virtue. The Religious Right has spent the past five decades teaching people that sure, we're all sinners—but look at *those* people's sins! A fierce, two-fisted battle posture has become so many evangelical Christians' default setting, the irony of which is not lost on so much of the watching world. They see the dissonance between a *blessed are the peacemakers* Jesus and these perpetual culture warriors, and they know something is terribly off.

And religious conservatives certainly haven't cornered the market on rightness tribalism. We left-leaning Christians are as prone to it as anyone, I'll admit; we're as equally susceptible to thinking our stuff doesn't stink. Though we advertise an attitude of openness and tolerance, to be honest that usually gets extended politically and theologically to the left of us but not to the right. We aren't as charitable to those who still reside in the orthodoxy we departed from, and definitely not to people who seem not only in opposition to us, but stridently so. As our faith evolves, it's really easy to slip into progressive arrogance: to be cynical about people who still believe what we once believed; to suspect them of insincerity or duplicity or ignorance because their convictions no longer match our own; to imagine ourselves enlightened minds positioned in the moral battlefield across from dim and darkened adversaries who don't know what we know. That's the dan-

HONORING OTHER PEOPLE'S JOURNEYS

GREATER COMFORT WITH DIFFERENCE

gerous irony in condemning someone for their spiritual close-mindedness while declaring them less evolved or intelligent or sincere than you are. You miss the mess of your own making.

I've always been strangely encouraged by Jesus' command to love my enemies—because it means I get to have enemies! Implied in that instruction is the realization that I don't have to agree with everyone or like everyone or get along with everyone. It means I can recognize people as fully adversarial to me and even push hard against them when our values differ—I just have to hold on to my soul and not lose my religion whenever I do. In Matthew chapter 7, when Jesus warns those of us aspiring to follow him in the ways of compassion and equity not to judge others unless we're willing to be held to the same standard, he isn't saying that we don't name injustice or call out malevolence in the world. He isn't forcing us into some phony *kumbaya* with whoever or whatever we see as harmful. He isn't asking us to soften our language or compromise our convictions in any way. He *is* making certain that we never imagine ourselves as solely capable of virtue or singularly immune from immorality; that we fiercely nurture humility regarding ourselves and mercy toward everyone else. Most of us don't like to do that because self-righteousness is far too intoxicating a drug and much too easy to become addicted to. Trust me, because I've been trying kick it for a long time—and that can be difficult when you're as right as often as I am. (I'm only slightly joking.)

I know why I believe what I believe. I take my faith seriously, and I've studied and reflected and prayed and learned and cared my way into the perspective that I have, and I imagine you have too. The greatest challenge we face in loving the entire world (not just the people in it that we like) is in believing that the people with whom we disagree have reached their present belief system as thoughtfully and prayerfully as we have. Part of not being a jerk in matters of belief is not assuming that simply because someone's conclusions don't align with ours that their journey is less valid or sincere or meaningful. For example, I firmly believe Jesus is what many professed Christians would mockingly call a *social justice warrior*: that he regularly engaged systemic brokenness in tangible ways, meeting needs and mending wounds and working to make the communities he existed in more equitable. I believe that if we try to have a Christianity without social justice, we cut out the beautiful, beating heart of Jesus and we are left with only a lifeless corpse of ceremonial religion to drag around. I believe that "justice" is what Jesus was doing and preaching and demanding of those who would follow him; and that justice is precisely what made the powerful want him dead. I also know that many devoted, sincere people of faith believe this is a reckless liberal distortion that distracts us from the true reason Jesus came: helping people avoid hell. They believe that my focus on social justice and away from sin management is a heretical, selective betrayal of the gospel that is dooming souls in my wake—and I think their preoccupation with eternity causes them to miss the needs of the people present with them. They find my fixation on this world as misguided as I find their obsession with the next one. They think faith is about saving people from eternal torment; I more often want to prioritize helping them escape the hell that's here. I don't have to agree with these people or win them over, but I'd better make sure I don't see their religion as lesser than mine—and most of us do this every day without realizing it.

If you're currently part of a faith community, have you stopped to consider why you're there? Likely, there are all sorts of reasons: family history, meaningful relationships, the children's program, the minister's sermons, the music, proximity, a ministry that connects with your heart—and ultimately, on some level you're there because you think they get something right about God. You have some affinity with however they imagine, talk about, and perpetuate the source of all things or you probably wouldn't be there; and you think that they have it more right than other communities you pass by on your way there. For years, I thought that one of my primary jobs as a pastor was getting people to buy into our church's *God box* and everything within it (which, of course, was carefully curated by myself and those on our staff), by convincing them that our particular box was better than any they'd encountered. Sure, it was a personal relationship with Jesus through the limitless power of the Holy Spirit—but an intangible God needed a physical house, and as far as that went, we'd built the best one. We'd told ourselves that love was the impetus (and of course, it was), but there was also a fair amount of subconscious hubris to imagine we'd cracked a code that to this point in human history has escaped every other church's previous efforts. There's an epidemic of such subtle arrogance.

For a long time, it never occurred to me how strange it was that within one square mile of us, dozens of faith communities of every tradition and variety were operating under the same flawed and oddly competitive premise that we were, and we were all trying to figure out how to pull the same people's attention from all those other God boxes to our obviously superior model. Even the purest of churches feels the same pressures to grow numerically, to gain market share, to get more buyers—all the churches I've ministered in have. It's hard to see that from inside, though. Like most ministers and lay leaders, we were working really hard to do good in the world and to meet the many demands on our time and bandwidth—and getting a second to step back and breathe and get some perspective wasn't usually an option. In the middle of launching ministries and planning events and getting rear ends in the seats, it was nearly impossible to interrupt the velocity and activity of our busy calendars and taxed schedules to actually get together with other churches (let alone communities well outside of our denomination or tradition or worldview) to compare our containers for God; to consider all our doctrines and stances and methods, our differences and idiosyncrasies; to benefit from one another's specific shared wisdom. If we had, I imagined we'd have walked away with a more expansive understanding of the scale and scope of the love that holds us all. This wouldn't have necessarily come from our points of agreement, but our numerous incongruities as well. If communities invested in collaborative compassion more often, they might even concede there are truths about God that are outside what they've imagined or were previously comfortable with.

Not long ago, I was leading a Q&A following a presentation I made in rural Georgia to a tiny, passionate blue dot of humanity existing in a decidedly MAGA red community. The modest wood-beamed church sanctuary was filled to overflowing with progressive Christians, local LGBTQ activists, members of Democratic political groups, and a healthy sprinkling of humanists, former Christians, and two disappointed people who mistakenly thought they were going to see Jon Lovitz. A woman in her early sixties, decked out in a denim jacket emblazoned with dozens of patches and buttons, a sort of liberal Technicolor dreamcoat, grabbed

GIVING UP ON
BEING RIGHT

THE POSSIBILITY
OF CONNECTION
WITH THOSE
WHO DISAGREE

the microphone. Though her voice began unsteady and barely audible, it soon rose into a mighty, thundering roar. "Sometimes," she bellowed, gathering momentum, "you just have to say, 'Right is right and wrong is wrong,' and we've got right on our side and we need to stop apologizing for it and let them deal with it, because goodness matters!" Applause erupted and cheers shot around the sanctuary like rainbow-colored bottle rockets. The woman's face remained unchanged in its intensity as the adulation of these strangers washed over her. She meant what she said, and she hadn't said it to receive kudos or be congratulated. She was simply wearing her bleeding heart on her faded denim sleeve and expressing the pent-up exasperation of decades of fighting for goodness in a place where it always seemed hopelessly outnumbered. She was a dedicated damn-giver pushed to the brink.

I'd never met this woman before, though by quickly surveying the assortment of slogans and platitudes adorning her jacket, I realized that she and I likely agree on most issues, and my first instinct was a hearty "Amen," which I provided—but when the last of the handclaps ceased, I paused and said, "That all sounds great: standing for what is right when it's on your side, and I *do* believe we're on the right side of history in the work of compassion and equality and diversity. I *do* believe MAGA Christianity has gotten Jesus almost entirely wrong and this movement bears almost no resemblance to him." I continued, "But right now, somewhere either across town or in a nearby city or in another state, there is an upside-down Bizarro World gathering of this one; with people who believe the opposite of so much of what we believe, wearing vastly different buttons on their jackets, with antithetical political affiliations and theological perspectives and media choices—and with a very different pastor than myself on the platform in front of them." I went on, smiling at the woman next to me, "And someone in that gathering just grabbed the microphone and shouted out the very words you have, with equal conviction about standing on the right side of history and about defending morality from evil, and a crowd of people assembled there, who are equally certain they have Jesus on their side, are passionately applauding her declaration." I paused and asked, "Are we equally in danger of being overconfident but wrong? Because we've certainly decided they are."

That's probably why, as much as the overconfident, self-righteous, coffee-shop disciples and the brimstone-breathing preachers and the finger-wagging relatives in my life really upset me, I always have a small reservoir of compassion—because I recognize a bit of myself in them. That's how personal morality and religious convictions tend to work. No one believes they're getting it wrong. Everyone is certain their cause is just, their motives are pure, and their character unimpeachable. Every one of us has a story we tell ourselves, and we've spent a lifetime crafting an ironclad defense for it. Most people don't willingly invest their lives (and their afterlives) in an error, and as a result everyone thinks their God is the best one, or they'd choose a different one. Many religious people think they're loving their neighbor even if their neighbor has doubts about that, and most of us fancy ourselves table flippers while presiding over tables that themselves could use some upending. Maybe we should check our halos and egos at the door.

Chapter 18
THE GOSPEL
ACCORDING TO YOU

I rarely get unsolicited, handwritten snail mail delivered to my home from people I don't know—and when I do it's often a wildly scribbled manifesto littered with profanity and spelling errors, detailing the severity of the hell I'm going to and the velocity with which I'll be heading there the moment I take my final breath on this side of hereafter (closed, of course, with the condescending assurance that my doomed-to-suffering soul is being fervently prayed for, as is my immediately desired repentance). One October afternoon in 2018, however, I stood in front of our mailbox, opened a small cream-colored envelope, and immediately recognized on the unlined, handmade pages inside the almost machinelike, precise cursive writing of what I suspected was an older person (as such penmanship is a disappearing art in most people younger than me). It was from a woman named Margaret. She'd read a recent article I'd published about evangelical Christianity's inexplicable alignment with the Trump administration and wanted to share her story with me.

As I slowly deciphered the tiny calligraphic lines and began to understand what they were excavating from the past, my hands started to tremble. Now ninety, Margaret was born in the Netherlands and lived several of her childhood years under Hitler's regime. Her father was a political prisoner who'd been held captive and tortured for ten months before eventually dying in the Dachau concentration camp. I took a deep breath and kept reading. She said she'd written to me because she saw a painful history she'd personally lived and suffered and grieved through, now appearing to repeat itself in the United States under the president at that time, and she was terrified. "The dehumanizing language he is using and the violence he is encouraging, and the open hatred of his followers, are bringing back disturbing memories I never wanted to relive, with some of the very same iconography and rhetoric," she wrote. "And the worst part of it all is that, once again, this is a movement of people who say they are Christians—and once again I don't understand."

Margaret asked me how such a thing could happen nearly one hundred years after the trauma she and so many millions endured, how people who say they love Jesus could again be so far from the heart of their original mission. I'm pretty sure Margaret was speaking rhetorically and wasn't really expecting a sufficient answer, which is fine because I couldn't give her one, at least not one that was worthy of her story. I couldn't and can't intellectually explain how so many people could get God so wrong and why that God will allow so many to get him/her/them wrong without sending some suitable attention-getter and making God's self clear.

Margaret asked me to "keep working for a Christianity that resembles Jesus," and this has been something I strive for every single day. It has, among countless other moments of my journey, honed my theology, informed my writing, and fueled my activism. I'm not going to suggest you need to agree with Margaret or my assessment of the recent theocratic movement in America echoing the horrors of history, but I am going to ask you to look at the world with fresh eyes and decide where it lacks love individually and systemically—and invite you into that vacancy because you are positioned and prepared to fill it, and because if you consider yourself a person of faith, morality, or conscience, that's the point of being here on the planet. We aren't forced to do such things, but we have the opportunity to choose to be agents of healing and restoration in the place and time in which we find ourselves and among the people we get to share space with. We get to leave a mark.

A decade ago, I was sitting in a church staff meeting when our children's pastor, Sharon, shared the ministry ceilings she'd reached in the denomination she grew up in because they wouldn't officially ordain her as a pastor. When others in the room responded in head-shaking disbelief, Sharon smiled widely, clapped her hands together, and said, "I don't need to be ordained, I'm anointed!" She knew her journey, her experience, her study, and her ministry spoke for themselves, and she believed that she'd been given everything she needed by God—and she was right. There was nothing she lacked that anyone else could give her, no credentials that were coming from a higher place than she'd already heard from. People might prefer such things in order to affirm her, but God didn't require them. She had as much as any of the disciples of Jesus had: a testimony and a voice. I bet you do too.

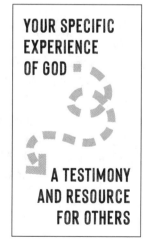

YOUR SPECIFIC EXPERIENCE OF GOD

A TESTIMONY AND RESOURCE FOR OTHERS

When I say the word *evangelist,* I imagine you picture a smooth-talking TV megachurch pastor, a pulpit-pounding brimstone-breathing minister, a bullhorn-wielding street preacher, or perhaps a white-haired grandfatherly religious elder figure—but unless you are in the ministry, I'm willing to bet you don't think about the person staring back at you in the bathroom mirror every morning. You really should, though. The word *evangelist* means "one who brings the good news," and it is closely tied to the word *gospel,* literally referring to the good news an evangelist brings—so in religious matters, the Bible tells us that the message and the messengers are inextricably and intimately connected.

This is true about you and me and whatever we're passionate about, though, isn't it? I've always joked that in addition to being a pastor, I'm also a food evangelist. There are few things I love more than driving around someplace I've never been, stumbling upon some roadside barbecue joint, hidden side-street trattoria, or random food truck, feeling as if I alone discovered it—and then taking to social media to publicly bear witness to the glory of this previously uncharted gastronomic wonderland in hopes of converting the uninitiated. (I wrote a book called *A Bigger Table,* after all.) These deep-fried, chocolate-covered, pork-fat-induced sermons are some of my greatest and most persuasive. Music has always been a similar source of passionate proselytizing. As a teenager, my fluent love language was the cassette mix tapes I'd meticulously put together for my classmates or my latest crush. In later years, this became home-burned CDs I handed out in my college dorm, and today the virtue manifests itself in the far less romantic but much less time-consuming act of sharing YouTube clips on my timeline—all in an effort to gloriously alter another human being's life with three chords and the truth in the way mine had been.

We're all preaching something we know to be true because we've experienced it. Dozens or perhaps hundreds of times a day, you loudly and explicitly share the gospel of your favorite team, a local restaurant you've come across, the gym where you work out, a weight-loss program you love, a new show you're streaming, a band you saw last night. In fact, your entire social media profile might be described as "The Gospel according to You." It's all the beauty, truth, meaning you've encountered and deemed worth sharing with the humanity around you. No one has the specific amalgamation of information you have, and that's why people connect with you on social media, why they call you when they're hurting, why they count you as a friend, why they share life with you: because they can't get *you* anywhere else. This is true in spiritual matters too.

You are the world's leading expert on your experience of God. You are the only one who can tell that story in the way you can tell it—and that is why your reading this book is important, as is what you'll do in response. Have you ever thought about what makes you different from your pastor? I can tell you from experience, it's very little: maybe a couple years of seminary, a reserved parking spot at a church, a website bio, and a group of people who sit and listen to them for an hour a week because of those other things. Beyond that, you are identical in what you have access to and are made of and can offer the world. The authors of the Bible's four biographies of Jesus, attributed to men named Matthew, Mark, Luke, and John, had three commonalities: their personal encounters with God, their front-row-seat accounts of interactions between humanity and the Divine, and their willingness to tell somebody. You have those things, too. Sure, you may not have accompanied an in-the-flesh Jesus walking through a field or enjoying a hillside meal or attending a wedding in need of wine—but you have access to the same God they did and were formed by the same Maker they were. The apostle says that same Spirit in Jesus is within you.[1]

The United Church of Christ has long used the tagline *God Is Still Speaking*, and that's only part of the story. If God is God, not only is God still speaking, but God is capable of speaking to and through each of us in ways that are entirely specific and fully unprecedented. It's a beautiful prayer to reflect on what good news you're bringing to the people you encounter in this life, what kind of gospel you've been preaching. That doesn't have to be an overtly religious idea or have a theological bent to it at all. The more elemental questions are, What are other people experiencing when their lives intersect mine? What is the net effect of my existence on humanity? Is it more or less loving, compassionate, and kind than when I arrived? It takes very little to tip the scales.

My Vote Common Good tour mates and I were spent. We'd finally reached the parking lot of the tiny Texas border-town church where we'd be staying that night, but that Friday had been one long week. Our beleaguered, aging tour bus had meandered through hundreds of nondescript, barren miles—and after one mechanical breakdown (and several emotional ones), we were ready for a rest and a nice meal, outside the cramped confines of the six-by-eight "living area" of the cabin in which we'd spent the last few days—and the fierce thunderstorm outside was postponing our plans. The rain pelted the roof so hard that we had to yell to be heard, and after sitting inside for twenty minutes hoping to wait it out, we decided to make a mad sprint for the building. It was only a couple hundred feet, but by the time we'd reached the unmarked back door of the church, frantically rung the bell, and been hurriedly ushered in, we were all well soaked, with all our dry clothes still packed up on the bus. The pastor began giving us a brief tour of the sanctuary where we'd be holding an event the next day, then looked at his watch and abruptly interrupted himself, saying, "Oh, it's almost time!" at which point the dozens of volunteers around us began buzzing with accelerated activity, as if instantly switched into a higher gear.

We'd arrived on a special night. Every Friday for the past few weeks, the church had been hosting groups of Latino families who'd been released from Immigration and Customs Enforcement (ICE) custody, offering them a home-cooked meal and a place to stop and rest, get a shower, receive some basic medical care, and wash their clothes before the next leg of their uncertain journey. A moment after the pastor's declaration, a horn sounded and someone from the doorway yelled, "They're here!" We all ran outside into the driving rain and quickly formed an impromptu receiving line, holding umbrellas like a makeshift canopy over the guests who stepped gingerly off their far more modest bus and into the church. They looked tired: not the kind of tired we thought we were when we'd arrived, but real, soul-draining, marrow-deep exhausted. I'd started to feel silly for thinking I'd had a long day or an uncomfortable journey.

The members of our group had been asked to serve as table hosts for dinner, with several of the newly arrived guests seated alongside us, our only instructions being to make them feel welcomed and comfortable. "Easy enough!" I naively thought to myself. Soon, a young man named Hector and his six-year-old daughter, Angelina, were led to the table. I stood, smiled, and motioned them to sit in the seats next to me. Approximately fifteen seconds after this moment I began silently scolding my younger self for not paying better attention in the two years of high school Spanish I'd taken and from which I could now retrieve nothing other than the words for bathroom and friend (which would not be easily woven into a suitable sentence). I could see my old teacher, Mrs. DeStefano, shaking her head at me from my ninth-grade classroom, and I felt a flop sweat on my forehead, as in the absence of actual Spanish words I proceeded to make the inexplicable decision to speak English words— only slower and louder. (This, of course, was not helpful.) Hector seemed sympathetic to my discomfort and appreciative of my efforts, and in response to his sweet, knowing smile, suddenly something changed in me. I looked at him father to father, and I immediately stopped worrying about entertaining him or "helping" him, and realized that given the hell they'd been through, I didn't need to do anything except be a kind and welcoming presence, as they'd had so few recently. That became my sole purpose. I somehow managed to construct a few awkward sentences, telling Hector how beautiful Angelina was, and drew a picture of a tiger on the placemat in front of her. She smiled as if surprised by the big cat that materialized before her, and I was happy to have figured out a way to connect with her. (At least my art classes paid off.)

We laughed and gestured and made a conversation work as best we could between us, each knowing the other's heart. I pulled up pictures of my daughter on my phone and showed them to Angelina. She said she was pretty. It was a very sweet moment, made even better when one of the Spanish-speaking church volunteers sat down with us and began to translate, and we could share a bit more of our stories around the table. As we did, I realized there were so many similarities between Hector and me. We both had work that we loved and took great pride in. We both had a faith that shaped and sustained us. We both were proud fathers with amazing daughters who gave us unthinkable joy. We both had dreams and plans and hopes for them and would do just about anything to make those goals a reality. The only real difference is that we'd been born in different places with different skin, and because of that our stories had diverged greatly—and for as much common ground as we found around that table, I knew the morning was going to return each of us to our "normal," which would be far easier for me than for him.

My heart broke for Hector and Angelina, in part because I realized that, in the eyes of so many professed Christians they'd encountered in their journey and who fill the nation they now call home, they weren't real human beings. They weren't the beautiful, breathing "least of these" that Jesus says he inhabits and calls us to love as we claim to love him. To so many who occupy pulpits and hold political office, they were the stuff of racist stereotypes and incendiary sermons, the faceless bogeymen of partisan media, cheap meme fodder for would-be wall-builders. But I was close enough to see the creases around Hector's eyes and the dimple in Angelina's left cheek, and I wished for the less-than-loving people in their path to know the human beings on the other end of the bad stories they have.

For a few hours, Hector, Angelina, and I got to be Jesus to one another. We got to be neighbors, and we were able to show each other the kindness of being individually seen and individually heard and personally cared for—and we changed one another's stories. The truth is, we get that opportunity a hundred times a day, whether we recognize it or not. I had no illusions that I was some heroic figure

THE GAPS AND INEQUITIES WE SEE

OUR PERSONAL INVITATION TO MOVE

deigning to stoop down and offer Hector and his daughter sympathy. I was just a dad sitting across from another dad, grateful to share space for a while.

I often wonder if he remembers me. I hope so. I hope I showed up in his story to remind him that he is loved. That's all faith worth anything to me is: showing up and trying to be a presence that helps and brings people hope and lessens their struggle and makes them feel seen.

Hector and Angelina have had a road made much more painful and stressful and difficult by people claiming to love Jesus, and that's not all right with me. I know it's not all right with Jesus. I don't think it's all right with you, either. And if it isn't, then we're going to have to work to make sure that we get the one thing right that we can't afford to get wrong, because it's the single antidote to all that afflicts us. Friend, if you aspire to be someone who perpetuates the greatest goodness in this world, as difficult and confounding and costly as it is, may we pursue the elusive, difficult, but so very loving God-work of *simply not being a jerk*. For God's sake and for the sake of hurting, exhausted, scared human beings around us, if we accomplish only one thing with our remaining days, let's love one another.

DISCUSSION GUIDE

Chapter 1: Unboxing God

1. Can you think of a specific time when you felt tension between your former religion and your current beliefs? What was the cause?
2. The author talks about wanting a faith that makes us better humans. Why does that often seem so difficult? Why does religion often bring out the worst in people?
3. Can you identify with Tiffany's feelings of being untethered as her faith shifted and difficulty came? What anchors you in hard times and painful circumstances?
4. The author describes a "holy moment" on the beach. Where, outside of a specifically religious setting, have you experienced a spiritual encounter?

Chapter 2: Scary Bedtime Stories

1. What are some of your earliest memories of God? How did your childhood shape your adult spirituality?
2. When you think about the character of God, what are some images or traits that come to mind?
3. The author talks about the fear prevalent in much of organized religion. Where do you see this manifested in yourself and others?

4. Why is it difficult to pray for our "daily bread"? How does fear make the present more difficult to enjoy or endure? Talk about the balance between feelings of scarcity and a God who provides.

Chapter 3: The Sh*t Is Never Getting Together

1. The author describes the illusion of certainty that can be problematic for religious people. Where have you experienced that intolerance?
2. The Missouri pastor was trying to keep their community intact while boldly engaging justice issues. Is this possible? How do spiritual communities balance serving those who are already there and standing with vulnerable people who are not?
3. Do you ever have impostor syndrome regarding your religious beliefs? Where do you feel the temptation to feel inferior to others?
4. How do you reconcile the mystery involved in spirituality? How comfortable are you in not knowing, and how comfortable do you think most religious people are?

Chapter 4: Thou Shalt Not Be a Jerk

1. The author speaks of everyone "playing hurt." How does this change the way you move through the world, view yourself, see the people you disagree with? How should it change spiritual communities?
2. Terry's story highlights the experience of many people who encounter cruel human beings preaching a God of love and, as a result, run from religion. What advice would you give to people like him?

3. Have you ever experienced peer pressure to believe, profess, or affirm something in order to remain part of a spiritual community? Is it difficult to express doubt or divergence in your community?

4. Think about or write a What I Believe statement, being as honest as you can and avoiding familiar religious words and platitudes.

Chapter 5: The Dude Abides

1. Many Christians grew up with a male image of God. If you did, was that ever a source of tension for you? When did you first feel conflict with that idea, if ever?

2. If you've been able to transition to a wider identity for God, how did you do that? What has been helpful in unlearning the old story?

3. The author talks about "personifying God." What names, roles, titles for God do you default to in your thinking? How do you think that shapes your feelings about yourself? (For example: If God is Father or Mother, you are a child. If God is a friend, you are a friend.)

4. What are your thoughts on the idea that God is nonbinary and transcends gender? Is that a difficult concept to embrace?

Chapter 6: Made in America

1. Why have so many Christians conflated God and country? What are the causes of nationalistic religion?

2. Knowing what you know about Jesus' life and teachings, how are they compatible or not compatible with the American Dream? With democracy? With capitalism?

3. The author says that the American Church is often the last entity to embrace social change. Do you agree with that? If so, why do you think that is? What needs to change?

4. How can people of faith avoid a story that favors their nation? Is that possible? How can American Christians avoid nationalism?

Chapter 7: Oh, Hell No!

1. Do you agree or disagree with the author's statement that the existence of hell seems "incompatible with the character of a God whose defining trait is love"?

2. How do you think your ideas and images of the afterlife shape your engagement with this one? What do you believe happens after your last breath here?

3. The woman at the dog park tells a familiar Christian story of "deserving hell" but being rescued by God. What are your thoughts on this perspective? Has that been your story? Is it still? If not, what changed?

4. The idea of hell is easily weaponized against other people. How do people of faith become confident in condemning others?

Chapter 8: Let Them Eat Cake

1. Why are expulsion and rejection so common in people claiming faith in Jesus? Why don't we see the "theology of pulling toward" that the author writes about?

2. Have you evolved in your theology of sexuality? If so, what brought about the shift, and how has it changed you?

3. Jesus spoke very little about gender identity and sexual orientation, and at great length about helping the vulnerable. Why do you think so many Christians invert this balance when it comes to their engagement with the world?
4. How do you respond to Christians who use the "love the sinner, hate the sin" justification for their treatment of LGBTQ people?

Chapter 9: Doppelganger God

1. Is it possible to avoid imagining a God who resembles us? If so, how?
2. The author talks about the lenses we view the world through. How can you make sure you're intentionally seeing the world through a different set of eyes? What are some practical ways to learn additional stories or to adjust your own lenses?
3. Do you tend to see Jesus more as a pastor or activist, as personal caregiver or system challenger? How might you benefit from leaning into another aspect of Jesus than the one that you usually default to?
4. Can you think or talk about a time when you got a better story about someone and it reshaped the lenses you see the world with?

Chapter 10: Good Book, Lousy Hammer

1. What are your thoughts on the phrases "Bible believing" and "biblical God"? How do you understand and engage with the Bible?
2. What image, verse, story, or idea from the Bible is particularly difficult for you to reconcile with your faith?

3. Do you agree with the author that most Christians who weaponize the Bible haven't actually read it?

4. Can anyone avoid cherry-picking from Scripture? If not, how do we find common moral ground?

Chapter 11: GodFundMe

1. Do you think God causes or allows natural disasters, health crises, and acts of violence in order to teach people? Talk about the implications of your answer.

2. Has someone ever tried to spiritually interpret difficult or painful circumstances for you? Was it helpful?

3. The author talks about his conflicted feelings about praying for healing. How do you understand intercessory prayer?

4. The phrase "everything happens for a reason" is a common one when trying to understand tragedies. Do you agree or disagree with that idea, and why?

Chapter 12: Inside Job

1. The author talks about the threats to the Church coming from Christians. Do you agree or disagree with that assessment?

2. How do you balance the merits of staying in a faith community and changing it from within with the benefits of leaving it to live more authentically?

3. If you once considered yourself a Christian but no longer do, what was it that began that shift?

4. What do you believe is the greatest misconception about Christians?

Chapter 13: A Semi-Pro-Life Movement

1. Have you evolved on the issue of abortion, and how has your faith shaped that change?
2. Do you agree with the author that many Christians who claim to be pro-life ignore much of humanity after birth because that is a much more costly activism? Why or why not?
3. Where do you see pro-life Christians not practicing a "pro-humanity" theology?
4. What is the greatest obstacle to developing a consistent pro-life ethic?

Chapter 14: Holy Ferocity

1. How do you reconcile anger and spirituality? How are they compatible or not compatible?
2. Aristotle's "anger filters" are useful in slowing us down and making us more self-aware. When do you most have difficulty slowing down and looking at your anger?
3. Can you think of a time when the way you were expressing your spiritual beliefs and moral convictions was described by someone as "angry"?
4. What makes you angry from a spiritual perspective? When do you feel that "holy ferocity" the author described?

Chapter 15: Love Your Damn Neighbor

1. The author talks about the influence of our "privilege bundle." How do you think yours has shaped your spirituality, your morality, or simply the way you see the world?

2. What systemic ills do you see the Church most failing to address? What ones does it address well?

3. Do you think you'd be capable of inviting people with divergent views into sustained relationship the way Susan did? What kind of people would be most difficult to invite?

4. The author describes looking back and noticing how his "set of assumptions about the world" was difficult to overcome, how he defended a story that he needed to be true even if it wasn't. Can you think of a difficult truth you've had to come to terms with and how it altered your theology or your expression of it?

Chapter 16: The Church of Not Being Horrible

1. If you were starting a Church of Not Being Horrible, how would it be different from most churches? Where would you start?

2. The author talked about the best spiritual communities being "recovery communities" where people can fail and fall and heal and be honest with their struggles. What prevents more churches from embodying that aspiration?

3. Belonging is a huge part of feeling loved. Where have you experienced that sense of "found-ness" the author writes about?

4. Do you believe a local church or in-person community is necessary for someone on a spiritual journey?

Chapter 17: High Horses and Better Angels

1. Have you ever thought about the competitive nature of faith communities, inside and outside their faith

tradition? How do you think that negatively impacts those specific congregations themselves and the bigger world outside of them?

2. Where have you noticed a feeling of superiority creeping into your spirituality? How do you look down on other people for what they believe or don't believe?

3. How might you find a way to engage in "collaborative compassion" with a group of people or a community whose beliefs are different from yours?

4. Can you think of someone who models humility in their beliefs when it comes to engaging others?

Chapter 18: The Gospel according to You

1. How does the idea of a "Gospel according to You" inspire, encourage, or anger you?

2. It's often easier for us to "evangelize" music, food, movies, or places than our spiritual beliefs. Why is that?

3. Think about three moments when you felt loved. Can you find any commonalities in those experiences?

4. Jesus' command is to love God, neighbor, and self. Which of these is the most difficult for you?

ACKNOWLEDGMENTS

I began writing this book in February of 2020. A few weeks later, the world turned upside down. I am eternally indebted to those who shared this journey with me, often from a distance; those who helped me keep my equilibrium, find the way forward, and stay focused on love.

To my wife, Jen, and my kids, Noah and Selah, for being the greatest traveling companions anyone could be fortunate enough to have. I am home with you.

To my amazing family: Mom and Dad, Brian, Eric, Michelle, Victor, Christopher, Beth, and Abigail. I am fortunate to have been born among you and be connected to you.

To my extended families, both by blood and in-law. Thank you for your love, presence, and kindness.

To the entire WJK family for continuing this journey with me. Your enthusiasm and trust is such an encouragement. Extra-special gratitude to my peerless editor, Jessica Miller Kelley. This book wouldn't have happened without you. Thank you for helping me say what needs to be said, and to say it better than I would have.

To my steadfast and stellar literary agent, Sharon Pelletier, and the entire Dystel, Goderich & Bourret LLC team, for partnering with me in this adventure since day one. You're amazing.

To my readers and followers, for being a beautiful extended family and for being the daily inspiration for this book.

To my Patreon supporters, for your partnership financially, emotionally, and spiritually. You have been invaluable in my life.

To all the church communities I have served, each one of them teaching and challenging me in profound, life-altering ways.

To everyone who has ever read, commented on, or shared my words. It is something I never take for granted.

To all those who believe that love will have the last, loudest word.

Patreon Community

A special thank you to these Patreon supporters for helping me keep saying stuff that needs to be said:

Alan Rajan Agarwal
Carl Angoli
Brittny Angwafo
Rosemarie Auten
Terry Baxter
Deborah A. Beal
Julie Beck
Judith Bessette, EdD
James Buckmaster
Patrick and Shauna Burgess
Andre Chasse
Carol Clayton
Donna Conner
Blaine Cressman

Shelby Day
Mike DeFino
Kathleen Durning
Jonathan Drummond
Rebecca M. Edwards
Erin Essenmacher
Michael A. Evans
Jenette Finch
Linda Finley
JoAnn Forsberg
Stacy Forte
Ann E. Garrett
Marianne Griebler
Grant Grissom

Susan Gutowsky
Suzi Herbert
Alan Heyman
Tommy Hickey
Karla Hollenbach
Linda D. Holy
Nicole Hopkins-Payne
Jimmy Janacek
Melanie Johnson
Pamela Little Johnson
Pamela Kampfer
Colleen Kane
Judy J. Kelly
Chris Knickerbocker
Debra Lambert
Katy Lightsey
Chris Lopez
Janice Lynn Luder
Susan Luhrs
Lydia Lee Martin
June McGraw
R. Mark Miedema
Walter Miller
Nancy R. Misner
Joni Mitchell
Elsie Mowins
Cindy Moy

Nanna Sally Nelson
Nysha Oren Nelson
Alex and Diana Nichols
Darla O'Connor
Vicki Palefsky
Valerie Peterson
Barbara Pfeiffer
Patrick Phillips
Steve Presley
Jeffrey Rathgeber
Kellie Rorrer
Carrie Rough
Landon Shultz
Vicki Stein
Laurie and Thomas Struck
Annette Tackett
David Tarrien
Gregory Tharp
James Townsend
Shawn Wakefield
Rod Wallace
Rev. Dr. Doe West
Bradley White
Jennifer Williams
Roy H. Williams
Jon and Anita Young

NOTES

Introduction

1. Matthew 22:35–40.
2. Matthew 7:1–5 NIV.
3. *The Matrix*, directed and written by L. Wachowski and L. Wachowski (Warner Bros., 1999).
4. Theodore Parker (1810–60), paraphrased in 1958 by Rev. Dr. Martin Luther King Jr., https://en.wikiquote.org/wiki /Theodore_Parker.

Chapter 1: Unboxing God

1. Ephesians 3:18–19 NIV.
2. Mark 2:21–22 NIV.
3. Matthew 5, Sermon on the Mount.

Chapter 2: Scary Bedtime Stories

1. When I use the masculine pronoun for God, it will be as used by others, not as a gender designation I make.
2. Luke 3:10–11.
3. Acts 2:42–47.
4. Matthew 6:9–14.
5. Luke 12:13–21.

6. Matthew 10:29–31.
7. 1 John 4:18.

Chapter 3: The Sh*t Is Never Getting Together

1. Psalm 139:1–6
2. Genesis 32:22–28.
3. "How Many Car Accidents per Day in the United States," *Amar Esq. PLLC* (blog), https://amaresq.com/blog/auto -accidents/how-many-car-accidents-per-day/.
4. Hebrews 11:1.
5. Matthew 5–7.
6. Mark 4:35–41.

Chapter 4: Thou Shalt Not Be a Jerk

1. Peter Lattman, "The Origins of Justice Stewart's 'I Know It When I See It,'" *Wall Street Journal*, September 27, 2007, https://www.wsj.com/articles/BL-LB-4558.
2. Mark 6:30–44.
3. John 8:7.
4. Mike Sager, "Tom Petty: What I've Learned," *Esquire*, October 2, 2017 (originally published August 2006), https:// www.esquire.com/entertainment/music/a889/tom-petty-what -ive-learned-interview/.
5. Luke 10:25–37.
6. Luke 24:13–35.

Chapter 5: The Dude Abides

1. *All in the Family*, "Archie's Helping Hand" (1974), https:// www.imdb.com/title/tt0509829/characters/nm0005279.
2. John Mark McMillan, "How He Loves," Integrity's Hosana! Music, 2005.
3. Hosea 11:3–4; Deuteronomy 32:11–12; Isaiah 42:14.

4. Matthew 7:21; Matthew 18:23–35; Matthew 25:14–30; Matthew 20:1–16; Matthew 21:28–32.

Chapter 6: Made in America

1. Daniel Cox, "White Christians Side with Trump," *PRRI*, November 9, 2016, https://www.prri.org/spotlight/religion-vote-presidential-election-2004-2016/.

Chapter 7: Oh, Hell No!

1. Matthew 13:49–50.
2. Psalm 42:7.

Chapter 8: Let Them Eat Cake

1. Masterpiece Cakeshop v. Colorado Civil Rights Commission (2018), https://www.supremecourt.gov/opinions/17pdf/16-111_j4el.pdf.
2. Brooke Sopelsa and Tim Fitzsimons, "Suit Filed against Christian School that Expelled Girl after Rainbow Birthday Photo," NBC News, January 24, 2020, https://www.nbcnews.com/feature/nbc-out/suit-filed-against-christian-school-expelled-girl-after-rainbow-birthday-n1122001.
3. Matthew 7:1–5.
4. Matthew 9:35–38.

Chapter 9: Doppelganger God

1. Luke 22:35–53.
2. Mark 10:6–8.
3. John 8:2–11.
4. John 10:1–21.
5. Luke 15:11–32.

Chapter 10: Good Book, Lousy Hammer

1. Genesis 3.
2. Genesis 6.
3. Joshua 6.
4. Book of Job.
5. John Pavlovitz, "No, the Bible Doesn't Say that Being LGBTQ Is a Sin (Getting Honest about Sexuality and Scripture)," YouTube video, May 13, 2020, https://www.youtube.com/watch?v=cgXwKVYBgSI.
6. Leviticus 20:9–10 NIV.
7. John 10:12.

Chapter 11: GodFundMe

1. Ed Mazza, "Kirk Cameron: Hurricanes Are Sent by God for 'Humility, Awe and Repentance,'" *HuffPost*, September 8, 2017, https://www.huffpost.com/entry/kirk-cameron-hurricanes_n_59b22199e4b0dfaafcf6d9a4.
2. *Crimes and Misdemeanors*, directed and written by Woody Allen (Orion Pictures, 1989).
3. Luke 18:1–8; Mark 2:1–12.

Chapter 13: A Semi-Pro-Life Movement

1. Aaron Rupar, "Trump Turns Shooting Migrants into a Punchline at Florida Rally," *Vox*, May 9, 2019, https://www.vox.com/2019/5/9/18538124/trump-panama-city-beach-rally-shooting-migrants.

Chapter 14: Holy Ferocity

1. Galatians 5:22–23.
2. Matthew 5:21–22.
3. Aristotle, *Nicomachean Ethics*, Internal Classics Library, http://classics.mit.edu/Aristotle/nicomachaen.mb.txt.

4. John 2:13–17; Matthew 23; Matthew 25:35; Mark 15:1–15.

5. Theodore Parker, paraphrased in 1958 by Rev. Dr. Martin Luther King Jr., https://en.wikiquote.org/wiki/Theodore _Parker.

6. Luke 4:16–21.

7. Luke 1:52–53.

Chapter 15: Love Your Damn Neighbor

1. Scrooge is reformed on Christmas Day in Charles Dickens's *A Christmas Carol* (1843).

2. Matthew 7:15–17.

3. Matthew 5:46.

Chapter 16: The Church of Not Being Horrible

1. *This Is Spinal Tap,* directed by Rob Reiner, written by Christopher Guest, Michael McKean, Harry Shearer, and Rob Reiner (Santa Monica, CA: Metro Goldwyn Mayer Home Entertainment, 1984).

2. Matthew 13:33.

3. Beit T'Shuvah, https://beittshuvah.org/.

4. Matthew 21:31–32.

Chapter 18: The Gospel according to You

1. Romans 8:1–17.